Kids FAVORITE Bible Stories

This Book Belongs to

_____

wonder kids
share the wonder

Table of Contents

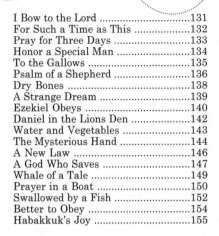

KIDS FAVORITE BIBLE STORIES
Bible stories retold by Stephen Elkins.

Published in Nashville, TN by Wonder Workshop, a division of Stephen's Group, Inc.

Scripture quotations used in this book are from the *New American Standard Bible* © 1960, 1977, 1995, by the Lockman Foundation; *The Holy Bible, New International Version* (NIV) © 1973, 1978, 1983, International Bible Society. Used by permission of Zondervan Bible Publishers; *The King James Version of the Bible* (KJV). Public Domain.

Illustrations by Tim O'Conner

Cover design by Kimberly Sagmiller, FudgeCreative.com; Jay Elkins, Wonder Workshop

Interior design by Kimberly Sagmiller, FudgeCreative.com; Jay Elkins, Wonder Workshop

ISBN 13: 978-1-56919-082-1

Printed in China

1109 – HZ – PO1331

Old Testament

In the Beginning

In the beginning God created the heavens and the earth. Now the earth had no shape or form, and darkness covered the waters. And the Spirit of God was present, passing over the waters.

And God said, "Let there be light." And there was light! God saw that the light was good, and He separated the light from the dark. He called the light "day" and the darkness "night." So ended the first day of creation.

6

"Let there be light."

God Makes the Sky

Then God said, "Let there be a visible arching sky that separates the water." So God made the sky to separate the waters under it from the waters above it. And everything that God spoke was accomplished in the power of His word. And so ended the second day of creation.

And God said, "Let the waters under the sky be gathered in one place and let dry land appear." And it was so. God called the dry land "earth" and the gathered waters "seas." And God saw it was good. Then God made every kind of plant and tree, and God saw that it was good. And so ended the third day of creation.

God Creates Two Great Lights

And then with His word, God created two great lights ... the sun to shine in the day and the moon to brighten the night. He also made millions of stars. God set them in the heavens to give light to the earth. And God saw that it was good. So ended the fourth day of creation.

God made the stars.

God Made the Birds

And God said, "Let the waters be filled with living creatures, and let birds fly through the skies." So God made creatures of every kind that live in the sea and every winged bird that soars above. And God saw that it was good and He blessed them. And so ended the fifth day of God's marvelous creation.

God Makes Man

And God said, "Let the earth produce wild animals, livestock, and all other creatures that walk or creep upon the ground." Then God said, "Let us make man in our image and let them rule over all creation." So God created man in His own image; male and female He created them. God blessed them and saw that all He had made was good. And so ended the sixth day. God had finished His work. So on the seventh day, He rested.

On the seventh day He rested.

Adam's Special Job

The Lord God used the dust of the ground to create Adam, the first man. When God breathed His breath of life into Adam's nose, he became a living soul.

The Lord placed Adam in a beautiful garden called Eden. It was a perfect home. Adam was given the special job of taking care of all God had made.

Adam was the first man.

11

Do Not Eat

Then the Lord said to Adam, "You may eat the fruit from any tree in the garden except one. Do not eat from that tree." And God warned Adam that if he disobeyed and ate the fruit, he would die.

So Adam did the things God asked him to do.

Adam obeyed God.

God Makes a Helper

Then the Lord said, "It is not good
for Adam to be alone. I will make him
a helper and friend." So the Lord caused
Adam to fall asleep. God then removed one
of Adam's ribs and from it He made a woman.
God brought the woman to Adam and he was very pleased.
Together Adam and Eve took care of the garden and
worshiped God.

Adam and Eve worshiped God.

Adam Names the Animals

Now the Lord created every beast of the field and every bird in the sky and brought them to Adam one by one. Adam gave each one of them a name.

He gave names to all the cattle, to the birds of the air, and to every beast of the field.

The animals came to Adam.

A Bad Choice

Now there appeared in the garden one day a serpent who had come to tempt Adam and Eve. He was very clever.

One day he found Eve alone in the garden near the forbidden tree and he spoke, "Did God really say not to eat from every tree in the garden?"

Adam and Eve were tempted.

15

Eve was startled and said to the serpent, "We may eat the fruit of every tree in the garden except this one. For God has warned us. He said do not eat this fruit or even touch it or we will die."

"You will not die!" said the serpent. "God knows that if you eat the fruit of this tree, you'll be just like Him!"

God said, "Don't eat."

The Forbidden Fruit

"Your eyes will be opened and you'll know about good and evil, and you'll be just as powerful as He is!" Even then gazed back upon the forbidden fruit. She remembered God's warning, but the serpent's words did seem to make sense. She could see with her own eyes that this fruit looked as ripe and sweet as any in the garden.

"This fruit looks good. It probably tastes good too. And wisdom is something everyone needs! The serpent is right," she thought. "God doesn't want us to be wise!" So Eve took the fruit and ate it. Soon, Adam came by and she gave the fruit to her husband. He ate it also. Adam and Eve had sinned against God.

"You'll be like God!"

Adam, Where Are You?

Soon they heard the voice of the Lord as He walked through the garden. "Adam, where are you?" He called. Adam answered, "We were hiding, Lord, because we were naked and afraid." Then God said, "Adam, have you eaten from the tree that I warned you not to?"

Adam answered, "The woman you made to be my helper, she gave me the fruit and I did eat."

"We were hiding, Lord!"

Then the Lord said to the woman,
"What have you done?"
"The serpent
confused me, Lord.
He told me I would
not die and that we
could be gods too!"
Adam and Eve were
afraid and ashamed of
what they had done.

Then God said to the serpent, "I curse you this day for what you have done. You will crawl on your belly all the days of your life."

The serpent fell silent on the ground and slithered away.

Adam and Eve were ashamed.

The Work Begins

The Lord said to Adam, "Because you disobeyed me, you shall work very hard for your daily bread. The ground will be full of thorns and thistles."

The Lord made them clothes to wear and sent them out of the Garden of Eden, never to return again. Behind them He placed an angel with a flaming sword to guard the entrance to Eden.

God made them clothes.

Noah's Ark

Many years had passed since the day Adam and Eve were forced to leave the Garden of Eden. The world was full of people who had become very wicked. They never prayed or thought about their heavenly Father. God's heart became full of pain and He was sorry He had ever created them. So the Lord said, "I will destroy these people whom I have created."

God was full of sorrow.

21

A Man Named Noah

But there was a man named Noah who loved the Lord with all his heart. When everyone else had become selfish and mean, Noah and his family walked with the Lord.

God was pleased with Noah and said, "I am going to send a great flood upon the earth to destroy every living thing. Only you and your family will be saved."

Noah loved God!

Noah Obeys

God told Noah to build a large
boat, called an ark, out of gopher
wood. The ark would have many rooms
and a roof over the top to keep out the water.
"The Lord said this ark should be 450 feet long, 75 feet
wide and 45 feet tall, and have 3 decks. Now we're going
to bring two of every kind of bird and beast, male and female,
into this ark." Noah did all that God had asked him to do.

God said, "Build an ark."

It's Going to Rain!

So Noah, together with his three sons Shem, Ham and Japheth, and his wife and his son's wives, built the ark. They brought plenty of food aboard for themselves and the animals to eat.

Soon, the animals came to Noah and were loaded into the ark two by two. Then God said to Noah, "Go into the ark, for it will rain in seven days." Noah did all the Lord commanded.

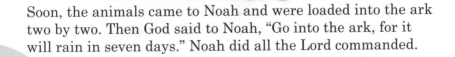

Animals came two by two.

Forty Days & Nights

Seven days soon passed. The skies darkened, the thunder crashed, and the rain began to fall. With two of every living creature aboard, God shut the door on Noah and his family.

It rained for forty days and forty nights. The waters rose higher and higher floating the ark high above the earth. Every living thing perished. Only Noah and those with him on the ark were safe.

Noah and the animals are safe!

Noah sends a Dove

The earth was flooded for 150 days. But God cared for
Noah and his family. He sent a warm heavenly
breeze to dry the earth. Soon, the ark came
to rest in the mountains of Ararat.
Noah waited 40 days before he
opened the window. He sent
out a raven, but there was
no dry place for the
bird to land.

Then he sent out a dove, but the dove could find no dry place
and returned to the ark. Noah waited seven more days before
sending the dove out again. This time the dove returned with
an olive leaf in its beak ... a sign that there was dry land.
Noah waited seven more days and again sent the dove out,
but this time the dove did not return.

The dove did not return!

Come Out of the Ark

Then God said to Noah, "Come out of the ark with your wives and your sons and their wives and all the animals." Noah was thankful God had saved his family, so he built an altar to please the Lord. "Thank you, Lord for saving my family. You are a wonderful God."

God made a promise never again to destroy the world with flood waters. As a sign of His promise, He set a beautiful rainbow in the sky.

God made a promise!

The Tower of Babel

After the great flood, Noah's children began to raise families. Their children had more children until the earth was one big family with one language. These families began to move eastward until they came to a place called Shinar.

There the ground was just right for making bricks and there was plenty of asphalt for mortar. They said, "Let's build a great city with a tower reaching to heaven."

So with bricks and tar the people of Shinar began building a tower to reach the very gates of heaven. When God came down and saw the tower, he was displeased. "These people believe they can build a tower that goes to heaven without calling on my name. Come, let us mix up their language so the people cannot speak to one another."

Mixed Up Language

Immediately, their language was confused and because they could no longer understand one another, the work stopped. The Lord scattered them over all the earth. That is why to this day we call this tower the Tower of Babel, for it was there the language was confused.

Abraham Believed God

God made three very important promises to Abraham.
One, God promised Abraham his own country.
Two, God promised Abraham children, even
though he was very old.
And three, God promised
Abraham that the
Messiah would
come from his
family.

Even though these were big promises, Abraham believed God
would do what He said! That is why he is called "the father of
all who believe." And yes, God kept his promises. Abraham's
country was called Canaan, his son was named Isaac, and the
Messiah was called Jesus!

God made three promises.

Sarah Laughs

Sarah was Abraham's wife. All her life she had wanted a child. Then, when Abraham was 99 years old, the Lord said, "I make you this promise: you and Sarah will have a son."

Sarah heard what the Lord said, and she laughed. After all, they were too old to have children. When the Lord heard her laughter, He said, "Is anything too hard for the Lord?" At age 90 Sarah had a son. They named him Isaac, which in Hebrew means, "he laughs."

Is anything too hard?

31

Esau and Jacob

Isaac loved the Lord and grew to be a great man of God. At age 40, he married a woman named Rebekah. Like Abraham and Sarah, they prayed that God would bless them with a child.

When Isaac was 60 years old, the Lord answered their prayers with a double blessing ... Rebekah was going to have twins! Even before the babies were born, Rebekah felt them kicking and fighting each other. "Why is this happening?" she asked the Lord.

Isaac loved the Lord.

Two Nations

The Lord answered and said, "Two nations are inside of you and the two will be separated. One will be stronger than the other; the older brother will serve the younger."

On the day of their birth, Esau, the first-born, was red and hairy. Jacob was fair and smooth and followed with his hand grasping Esau's heel. Just as Rebekah had been told, the two boys were very different.

The two boys were different.

A Pot of Stew

Esau grew up to be a very skillful hunter, while Jacob liked to stay close to home. One day Esau came home weary and tired from a long day's hunt. Jacob had just finished cooking some tasty stew. Esau was very hungry when he said, "Jacob, let me have some of your stew." Jacob replied, "First, sell me your birthright." This meant that Jacob, the second born, would have all the special honors given to the first-born.

Again, Jacob said, "Give me your birthright and I will give you food." Esau, being so tired and with the smell of Jacob's stew tempting him, replied, "I'm about to die anyway. What good is a birthright if you're dead of hunger. You can have it! Now, give me some stew!"

"Swear to me first," Jacob demanded. So Esau swore before the Lord and gave Jacob his birthright. How foolish he was to sell his birthright for so little!

"Sell me your birthright."

Give Me Your Blessing

Many years passed and their father Isaac became very old and blind. Fearing he may die soon, he called for Esau and said, "Take your bow and arrow to the country and bring back some wild game. Prepare a meal just the way I like it and bring it to me. Then I will give you my blessing."

When Rebekah heard what Isaac had said to Esau, she called for Jacob. She told Jacob she had a plan to trick Isaac so that he would be the one to take the food to Isaac and receive the blessing. Jacob was concerned Isaac would know.

Rebekah had a tricky plan!

He said to his mother, "Esau is hairy and I am not. What if father touches me and finds out I am not Esau? What if he curses me instead of blesses me?"

"The curse will be upon me," Rebekah said. "Now do as I tell you!" Then Jacob dressed in Esau's clothes and with his hands covered with goat skins, took the meal into his father's room.

Jacob dressed in Esau's clothes.

It's a Trick!

Jacob said, "The Lord God has given me a successful hunt. Rise and eat and give me your blessing." Isaac said, "Come close so I may touch you to know if you are really Esau."

When Isaac touched the hairy goat skin hands and smelled Esau's clothes, he blessed him saying, "May all people bless and serve you. May nations bow down to you." Now Jacob had taken Esau's birthright and blessing.

Just as Jacob left, in came Esau with the tasty meal he has prepared for his father. "Rise and eat and give me your blessing," Esau said. "Who are you?" Isaac asked. "I am your first-born son, Esau," he answered. Isaac trembled, "Who was it then that brought me food and received my blessing? For he will be blessed indeed."

Isaac blessed Jacob, not Esau!

He Has Taken
Your Blessing

When Esau heard his father's words, he cried, "Bless me, too, Father. Bless me, too!" Isaac raised his head and said, "Your brother has deceived me. He has taken your blessing and I have made him lord over you and all his relatives. I can give you nothing."

Esau hated Jacob and said to all, "The day is coming when I will kill Jacob."

"Bless me too, Father!"

Jacob's Stairway to Heaven

One evening on the way to Haran, Jacob stopped to rest for the night. He spread his blanket across the ground and used a large stone for a pillow. He fell asleep and dreamed he saw a stairway to heaven. The bottom of the stairway rested on the earth, the top reached to heaven. And the angels of God were climbing up and down the heavenly stairway.

Angels climbed the stairway.

A Promise Is Made

There above the stairway stood
Yahweh, our Lord, and He said,
"I am the Lord, the God of Abraham,
your grandfather, and the God of
Isaac, your father. I make this promise to you.
I will give to you and your children this land
where you are now sleeping. All the people on earth
will be blessed because of you and your family. I will
watch over you and no matter where you go, I will be
with you."

"Yahweh is our Lord."

Jacob woke up frightened.
"Surely the presence of the
Lord is in this place and I didn't
know it," he said. So early the next
morning Jacob arose and took his stone
pillow and poured oil over it and set it as
a reminder to the whole world that God had
been there.

Then Jacob made a promise to God. "If God will
watch over me on this journey and I return safely to
my father's house, then Yahweh the Lord will be my
God and I will give Him a tenth of all I may own."

God's presence is here.

Joseph: God Put a Dream in My Heart

Some years later, Jacob married and had twelve sons. He settled in a place called Canaanland where his sons tended flocks of sheep.

Now Jacob had a favorite son named Joseph who was born when Jacob was very old. To show his great love, Jacob made Joseph a coat of many colors. Many times Joseph would come to his father and tell him the bad things his brothers were doing. This made his brothers very angry and jealous.

Bundles of Grain

Joseph's brothers hated him for this and could not speak a kind word to him. One night the Lord sent Joseph a very special dream.

The next morning Joseph told his brothers all about it. He said, "We were in the fields tying bundles of grain together when suddenly my bundle rose up and stood tall while your bundles gathered around mine and bowed down to it."

The grain bowed down.

The Stars Bow Down

"Do you think you will someday rule over us?" his brothers said. And they hated him even more.

Then Joseph had a second dream. He said to his brothers, "This time the sun, the moon, and eleven stars were bowing down to me." When he told the dream to his father, Jacob was very unhappy. "Do you believe that your mother, and I, and your eleven brothers will bow down before you?"

"Will we bow down to you?"

A Plot Against Joseph

One day Jacob said to Joseph, "Your brothers are tending to our flocks near Shechem. Go to them and make sure all is well."

Joseph obeyed his father and soon found his brothers on a hillside. But his brothers had seen Joseph's coat of many colors from a distance, and before Joseph reached them, they plotted to kill him.

Make sure all is well.

Thrown in the Pit

"Here comes the dreamer," they said. "Let's kill him and throw him into one of these empty water holes and say a wild animal attacked and killed him. That will put an end to his dreams!" When the oldest brother Reuben heard their plan, he stopped it. "Do not kill him. Throw him into the pit, but do not harm him."

When Joseph saw his brothers, he ran to them. Suddenly, they all jumped on him and began tearing the coat of many colors from his back. They tied him up and threw him into an empty water hole. As they sat to eat, a caravan bound for Egypt passed by. Judah said, "Why don't we sell Joseph to these merchants. Then we'll be rid of him forever!"

A caravan passed by.

Joseph is Sold

Joseph was sold as a slave to the merchants for twenty pieces of silver. When Reuben found out what they had done, he said, "How can we face our father having done this?"

They decided to kill a young goat and dip Joseph's coat in the blood. They took the coat to their father and said, "Father we found this coat on our journey back home. Is it Joseph's?"

They took the coat to their father.

Jacob knew it was Joseph's coat and cried out, "It is Joseph's coat! Some wild animal has killed my son! He must have been torn to pieces."

Then Jacob tore his clothes and wept bitterly. No one was able to comfort him. Meanwhile, Joseph was on his way to Egypt.

Affirmation: I will not be jealous of others!

Most Trusted Servant

When the merchant caravan reached Egypt, Joseph was sold to an Egyptian named Potiphar who worked for the king as captain of the guard. Being an honorable man, Joseph soon became Potiphar's most trusted servant. Joseph even lived in Potiphar's house and was put in charge of all he owned.

Potiphar's wife became angry with Joseph because he would not disobey the law of the Lord. She said things about Joseph that were not true. Because of her lies, Potiphar had Joseph put in prison.

Joseph would not disobey.

Joseph Goes to Prison

Sometime later the king's baker and servant were also put into the same prison. Joseph took care of them. While they were there, each one had a dream which troubled them greatly. Joseph noticed their sad faces and asked, "Why are you so sad?"

"Last night, we both had strange dreams and we don't know what they mean," they said. "God knows everything," answered Joseph. "With His help, perhaps I can explain the dreams to you." The king's servant spoke first. "I saw a vine with three branches which budded and blossomed into ripe grapes. The king's cup was in my hand, so I squeezed the grapes into the cup and put the cup into the king's hand."

Joseph explained, "The three branches are three days. In three days the king will call for you and you will once again be his chief servant. When this happens, please mention me to the king and get me out of this prison, for I have done nothing wrong."

Joseph explains a dream.

The King is Troubled

The chief baker spoke up. "In my dream, on my head were three wicker baskets. The top basket was full of bread for the king, but the birds were pecking the bread to pieces." Joseph said, "The three baskets are three days. In three days the king will have your head cut off and hang you on a tree, and the birds will eat your flesh."

Everything happened the way Joseph said it would. The servant was freed, but the baker was killed. Two years passed and the king had a troubling dream. He called the wisest men of Egypt to explain it, but they could not.

Then the king's servant remembered Joseph and how Joseph had explained his dream while he was in prison. He spoke to the king. "There was a Hebrew slave named Joseph I met in prison who once explained the meaning of my dreams to me. All that he said came to pass. Perhaps he will know the meaning of your dream."

The king sent for Joseph and said to him, "I am told that you can explain the meaning of my dreams … is this true?" Joseph answered, "I cannot, but my God can. He will give you the meaning of your dreams."

The King sends for Joseph.

Cows by the Nile

The king told Joseph of his dream.

"I was standing by the Nile River when I saw seven fat cows come out of the water. Then seven skinny cows came out of the water. Then the skinny cows ate up the fat cows, but no one could tell they had eaten. Then I woke up."

Then seven skinny cows came.

Seven Years

"Later, I had a second dream where I saw seven ripe and healthy heads of grain growing on a single stalk. There sprang up seven more heads of grain, but these were withered and thin. Then, the seven thin heads of grain swallowed up the seven healthy heads. Is your God able to tell me the meaning of these dreams?"

Joseph answered, "God has indeed made known to you what He is about to do. The dreams are one and the same. The seven fat cows and the seven healthy heads of grain are seven years. The seven skinny cows and the seven withered heads of grain are also seven years. God has shown you that there will be seven years of plentiful food followed by seven years of famine and starvation. You should put a wise man in charge of saving up a part of the harvest in the good years to be eaten in the bad years."

The king thought Joseph's idea was very good, so he made Joseph second in command over Egypt to carry out the task of storing food for the coming famine.

"Is your God able?"

Joseph: Father and Son Reunion

Just as Pharaoh's dream had foretold, there were seven years of plenty. Joseph gathered a portion of the grain and stored it in the cities.

Then came the seven years of famine. The people cried out to Pharaoh for food.

Joseph then opened the storehouses of grain and there was plenty of food.

Go and Buy Grain

In Canaan where Joseph's father and brothers lived, there was very little food. Jacob told his sons, "I have heard there is plenty of food in Egypt. Go there to buy grain." And so ten of Jacob's sons left for Egypt. Benjamin, the youngest son, stayed with his father.

When the ten brothers arrived in Egypt, they were presented to Joseph. They bowed down to him with their faces to the ground. Joseph knew they were his brothers, but he pretended not to know them. He spoke harshly, "Where do you come from?"

"From Canaan," they replied. "We've come to buy grain." Then Joseph remembered the dreams he had about them.

They bowed down to Joseph!

You Are Spies!

"You are spies," Joseph said.

"No, my lord, we are the twelve sons of Jacob. The youngest is with him now, and we do not know where our other brother is."

"You are spies!" Joseph repeated, "and you will be tested!"

Then he put them in prison.

"Put them in prison!"

Bring the Youngest Brother

Three days later Joseph said, "One of you must stay here in this prison. The rest of you will return to your father's house.

Take this food to your starving family, but you must bring your youngest brother back to me. Then I will know you are telling the truth, and you will not die. Now, go!" Then Joseph had his brother Simeon bound before their eyes.

"Take this food to your family."

What Is God Doing?

Secretly, Joseph ordered his servants to fill their bags with grain and to put the money they had used for payment back in their bags. After this was done, the nine brothers started home.

Evening came and Joseph's brothers stopped to rest for the night. As they opened their grain sacks to feed the donkeys, they were frightened to find their own money. "What is God doing to us?" they asked. And they were afraid.

Soon, they arrived in Canaan and they told their father the things that had happened. "We must return to Egypt with Benjamin," they said. "No!" Jacob shouted. "Joseph and Simeon are gone and I will not allow Benjamin to go."

But when Jacob and his family had eaten all the grain, he knew that Benjamin would have to return with his brothers to Egypt to buy more grain if they were to survive. They prayed that God would be with them.

This time, they hurried down to Egypt taking with them special gifts for Governor Joseph. When Joseph saw them coming with his brother Benjamin, he said, "Servants, prepare a meal for these men." Then he left.

A Gift from God

Joseph's brothers were afraid. They thought
they might be put in prison for stealing,
so they tried to return the money
they had found in their bags to
Joseph's servant.

But the servant said, "Do not be
afraid. The money you found
was a gift from God."

"Do not be afraid."

The Silver Cup

Joseph had Simeon brought to them, and when he returned they gave him the gifts they had brought. Again, they bowed down before Joseph. As Joseph spoke to Benjamin, his heart was deeply moved with love. But Joseph still did not tell them who he was.

When the meal ended, Joseph ordered his servants to fill their grain bags to overflowing and again put each man's silver in their bags. Then he said, "Be sure to put my silver cup in Benjamin's sack." His servants obeyed.

When morning came, his brothers left for Canaan with the bags of grain. Shortly thereafter, Joseph sent his servant after them and he said, "My master was good to you. Why have you repaid him with evil and stolen his silver cup?"

They bowed to Joseph again.

Surprise, Surprise!

"We have stolen nothing," the brothers answered. "Search our bags. If you find the silver cup, the owner of that bag will die and we will become your master's slaves." So they each lowered their bags to the ground and opened them. The servant pretended to search each bag and found the silver cup in Benjamin's bag, right where he had put it. The brothers were surprised and could not believe it! They loaded their donkeys and returned to the city.

One Will Stay

They went into Joseph's house and bowed down before him terrified they would be put to death. Judah spoke, "God is punishing us for a terrible thing we did long ago. Now we are your slaves and Benjamin is at your mercy."

But Joseph said, "I cannot do such a thing to you. Only the one who has stolen my cup will stay here. The rest of you must go back to your father in peace."

"God is punishing us."

I am Joseph!

Judah walked closer to Joseph and said, "My lord, if Benjamin remains here, I am certain our father will die of a broken heart. He especially loves Benjamin as he did our other brother. Please take me in his place and let Benjamin return to our father."

When Joseph heard this, he could no longer hold back the tears. "I am Joseph!" he shouted. "I am Joseph, the brother you sold into slavery." His brothers were frightened and could not believe it was him.

Then Joseph said, "Come close to me, and do not be angry with yourselves. It was God who sent me here ahead of you to save you and your children from the famine. You intended to harm me, but God intended it for good."

God intended it for good!

Jacob Arrives in Egypt

Joseph then sent for his father Jacob. When Jacob arrived in Egypt, Joseph embraced him. Jacob said, "Now I can die in peace, for I have seen my son." Jacob and all of his family moved to Egypt where they lived for many years.

Joseph hugged his father!

Baby Moses

Many years later, after Joseph and all his brothers had died, Pharaoh was the new king of Egypt. He feared the children of Jacob, now called Israelites. "The Israelites are growing too strong," he said. "If there is a war, they may fight against us and defeat us."

To keep this from happening, he made the Israelites into slaves and put Egyptian masters over them. They were forced to work very hard making bricks and mortar.

They made bricks and mortar.

She Makes a Basket

Pharaoh used the bricks to build great cities. But no matter how unkind the Egyptian slave masters were, or how hard their work became, the Israelites continued to grow in number. Pharaoh became so angry he passed a cruel law ordering every baby boy born to an Israelite family to be drowned in the Nile River.

Now it happened that a baby boy was born to an Israelite family. Fearing Pharaoh's decree, the mother hid the baby for months. But when he began to cry and move about, she had to do something to save him. She decided to make a large basket out of the reeds that grew near the river. She sealed it with sticky tar so it would float.

She sealed it with tar.

Baby in the Reeds

Then she put the baby in the basket and set it among the reeds along the riverbank. His sister, Miriam, stood at a distance to watch over the baby.

That evening, Pharaoh's daughter went down to the river to bathe. It was then she noticed the strange basket floating among the reeds. "Fetch that basket," she said to her servant girl. When she opened the basket and saw the little baby boy, she loved him.

She loved him!

Son of a Princess

Then Miriam came forth and said, "Would you like for me to get an Israelite woman to take care of the baby?" "Yes, I would," said the princess.

So Miriam ran back to get her mother and told her the things that had happened. "Take care of this baby and bring him back to me when he is older," the princess said.

When the child grew older, his mother took him to Pharoah's palace, back to the princess, and he became her son. The princess named him Moses saying, "I drew him out of the water."

The Princess named him Moses.

A Slave Master Killed

Moses grew up in an Egyptian palace, but he knew he was an Israelite by birth. One day he went out to see how his people were being treated. He saw an Egyptian beating an Israelite worker. Moses had pity on the worker and tried to stop the beating. In anger, Moses killed the slave master and hid his body in the sand.

In time, Pharaoh found out what Moses had done. He declared that Moses must die. So Moses fled to the land of Midian.

Moses fled to Midian.

Words from a Burning Bush

One day while Moses was leading his sheep to Horeb, also called "the mountain of God," an angel appeared from within a burning bush.

Moses thought it was very strange that this bush, though on fire, did not burn up. Then God spoke to Moses from within the burning bush. "Moses, Moses," He said. "Here I am," Moses answered. "Do not come any closer. Take off your sandals, for the place you are standing is holy ground. I am the God of Abraham, the God of Isaac, and the God of Jacob." When Moses heard this he was afraid to look at God, so he hid his face.

"I have heard the cries and prayers of My people in Egypt. So go now. I am sending you to Pharaoh to free My people and lead them out of Egypt into a good land, a land flowing with milk and honey." But Moses said to God, "Who am I that I should lead the Israelites out of Egypt?" God answered, "I will be with you."

"Who shall I tell them sent me?" Moses asked. God answered, "I AM that I AM. Tell them I AM sent you."

"Tell them I AM sent you."

Moses asked, "What if they do not believe me? What if they will not listen?" Then God commanded Moses to throw down his staff. Moses obeyed and suddenly the staff became a snake. As Moses took hold of the snake, it turned back into a staff.

The staff became a snake.

Send Someone Else

Then the Lord spoke to Moses again, "If they do not believe you, take some water from the Nile River and pour it on the ground. It will become blood." But Moses did not want to go and spoke again. "O Lord, I don't speak very well, and my speech is slow. Please send someone else."

This angered God and he said, "Your brother Aaron speaks very well. He will go with you. Tell him what to say and he will say it."

So Moses and his brother Aaron left for Egypt.

Affirmation:
I will go where
God sends me!

Moses and Aaron left for Egypt.

Let My People Go!

Moses and Aaron arrived in Egypt and went to see the Pharaoh. Moses said, "The Lord God of Israel says 'Let My people go, so that they may celebrate their deliverance and worship Me in the desert.'" Pharaoh said to Moses, "I do not believe in your God and I certainly will not obey Him. The slaves are mine and I will not let them go."

"I will not obey your God!"

No More Straw

Then Pharaoh gave an order to the slave masters. "Do not give the Israelites any more straw for making bricks. Make them gather their own straw after they have finished working. But I want the number of bricks they make each day to be the same." This made their work even harder. Soon, the Israelites were beaten for falling behind in their work. Moses prayed, "O Lord, why have You brought more trouble upon Your people?" Then the Lord answered, "Because of My mighty hand, Pharaoh will let My people go. Tell My people that I am Yahweh, the Lord, and I will bring them out of bondage. They will be free and I will lead them to the land I promised Abraham."

Then the Lord said to Moses, "Go back to Pharaoh and tell him to let My people go! I will harden his heart so that he will not listen to you. But through it all, I will show Egypt that I am the true and living God. I will bring many hardships on them and soon the Israelites will be free."

Moses and Aaron returned to Pharaoh's palace and proclaimed, "The Lord has said, 'Let My people go.' Obey the Lord!" Then Aaron threw down the staff of Moses before Pharaoh and it became a snake. Pharaoh called for his magicians. When they threw down their staffs, they also became snakes. But they were amazed as Aaron's staff swallowed up theirs. But just as the Lord had said, Pharaoh would not listen.

"You will be free!"

The River Turns to Blood

God brought many unpleasant things upon the Egyptian people because Pharaoh would not obey God. First, Aaron dipped Moses' staff into the Nile River and it turned to blood. All of the fish died and the smell was terrible. No one could drink the water.

No one could drink the water!

Frogs Are Everywhere!

Seven days later Moses returned to Pharaoh and said, "The Lord says, 'Let My people go.' If you do not, I will fill the land with frogs. They will be in every house, even in your beds." Pharaoh said, "I will not free the people." So Aaron stretched out his hand with the staff, and there were frogs everywhere.

"Moses, pray that these awful frogs go away and I will let the people go," promised Pharaoh. So Moses cried out to God and the frogs went away. But Pharaoh broke his promise and did not let the people go.

Pharaoh broke his promise.

More Plagues Are Coming

"Let my people go!" cried Moses, but Pharaoh would not. So Aaron struck the ground with Moses' staff and tiny little gnats began to bite the Egyptians. Then the Lord sent swarms of flies to plague the Egyptians. They covered the entire land of Egypt, but there were no flies swarming near the Israelites.

"Moses, pray that these flies go away and I will free the people," promised Pharaoh. Moses asked the Lord to remove the flies, and God answered his prayer. But Pharaoh would not let the people go.

"Let my people go!" cried Moses, but Pharaoh would not. So the Lord sent a terrible disease that caused the horses and donkeys and camels, even the cattle and sheep to die. Then painful boils broke out on the Egyptians and their animals.

Then Moses stretched out his staff towards the sky and the Lord sent a terrible storm. There was thunder and lightening, and hailstones falling in the fields causing their crops to be beaten down. "Moses!" cried Pharaoh. "We have had enough! I will let the people go. Now pray that this terrible storm may go away." Moses knew Pharaoh would not keep his word, but to show God's power, he prayed and the stormy weather went away.

"We have had enough!"

Look at the Locust

Then Moses returned to Pharaoh's palace and said, "How long will you refuse to obey the Lord? Let my people go! If you refuse, locusts will cover the ground so it cannot be seen. And they will eat every green plant left by the hailstones."

"No!" shouted Pharaoh. So Moses stretched out his staff and locusts came and covered the ground until it was black. They ate everything growing in the fields and nothing remained.

They ate everything growing.

Total
Darkness

Pharaoh again called for Moses. "I have sinned, forgive me. Now pray to your God to take away these deadly locusts." Moses prayed to the Lord and a strong wind carried the locusts into the Red Sea. Not a single locust was left anywhere in Egypt. But Pharaoh would not let the children of Israel go. The Lord said, "Stretch out your staff toward the sky so that darkness will cover the land." Moses obeyed. For three days total darkness covered all of Egypt, yet the Israelites had light in their homes.

Moses again said to Pharaoh, "The Lord says, 'Let my people go!'" But Pharaoh was angry and he would not change his mind. "Get out of my sight, Moses and don't you ever come back here again. If you do, I will kill you!"

The Lord said to Moses, "I will send one more plague upon Egypt. Then Pharaoh will let my people go." Moses warned Pharaoh of a final plague. "The Lord has said, 'At midnight, I will go throughout Egypt and every first-born child will die. And a great cry will come from the people.' Your rulers will bow before me saying, 'You and the Israelites must go now.'" Then Moses left Pharaoh's palace angry that Pharaoh refused to listen to God.

A great cry will come from the people.

The Passover

THE PASSOVER

Exodus 12:13 ...and when I see the blood, I will pass over you.

The Lord told Moses and Aaron how to prepare for the last plague. "Tell My people that on the tenth day of this month, each household is to select one perfect lamb. Take care of it for four days and then kill the lamb at twilight. Take some of the lamb's blood and smear it on the sides and top of your doorposts. That night, you are to eat the lamb in haste, for it is the Lord's Passover.

On that night, the Lord will pass through Egypt. But when I see the lamb's blood on your doorposts, I will pass over you. You are to remember this day forever, and celebrate your freedom."

At midnight the death angel came and all the first-born in every household in Egypt died, even Pharaoh's son. But no one died in the Israelite homes with the blood smeared over the door. Pharaoh cried to Moses, "Go! Leave as fast as you can before we all die." The Israelites were free at last.

"I will pass over you."

The Red Sea Miracle

Six hundred thousand men, plus women and children, set off for the promised land. To guide Moses and the Israelites, the Lord sent a huge pillar of clouds to follow during the day, and a great pillar of fire as a guiding light by night.

Off to the Promised Land!

As soon as the Israelites left Egypt, Pharaoh's heart was quick to change his mind once again. "What have we done? We must capture the Israelites so they can work for us again."

Pharaoh took six hundred of his fastest chariots and an army of soldiers to capture the Israelites. As Moses reached the shores of the Red Sea, the Israelites saw the army coming. They were terrified. "We will die here in the desert," they cried.

Moses shouted,
"Stand firm!
Do not be afraid.
The Lord will fight for you."
Then Moses lifted his staff and
the seas parted. It was a miracle!
The children of Israel walked
through the sea with the walls of
water all around them.

They walked through the sea.

Broken Wheels

The Egyptian army followed Moses into the wall of water. But when morning came, the Lord threw the Egyptian army into confusion. The wheels on their chariots broke.

When the Israelites reached the other side, Moses stretched out his staff over the Red Sea. The powerful waters crashed down on top of the Egyptian army. They were defeated. Then the people of Israel put their trust in God.

The powerful waters crashed down.

The Long Journey

With the Egyptian army defeated by the Lord, the Israelites began their long journey through the wilderness. They were filled with joy and bound for the promised land. The people feared God and trusted Moses, His servant.

The wilderness was a very harsh and dry place, but the Lord provided sweet water to drink. Each morning the Lord rained down bread from heaven called manna. The people gathered it in baskets, enough for each day. It tasted like wafer cookies made with honey!

After three months of travel, the group reached Mount Sinai where they made camp. Then Moses went up the mountain where the Lord spoke to him. The Lord said to tell the people of Israel to obey His rules. Then they would be His special people, a holy nation. Moses returned to the people and told them what God had said. The people agreed to do all the Lord had commanded.

The Lord Is Coming

The Lord said He would
come before the people in
a thick cloud. Everyone would hear
Him speak and always trust Moses. He told Moses to have
the people wash and make themselves clean, for in three
days He would come down to Mount Sinai.

On the morning of the third day, there was thunder and
lightning. Then a thick cloud came over the mountain and
a very loud trumpet sounded. Everyone was afraid.

A thick cloud came over the mountain.

Up on the Mountain Top

Then Moses led the people to meet with God at the foot of the mountain. It was smoking like a furnace and the whole mountain shook. Moses called out and God answered.

God called Moses to the top of Mount Sinai and spoke these words, "I am the Lord your God who brought you out of Egypt." Then He gave Moses the Ten Commandments.

He gave Moses the 10 Commandments.

THE TEN COMMANDMENTS

1. You shall have no other gods but Me.
2. You shall not worship anything you make with your hands that looks like a creation of Mine.
3. You shall not use the name of the Lord to swear or curse.
4. You shall keep the Sabbath Day holy.
5. Honor your father and your mother.
6. You shall not commit murder.
7. You shall not commit adultery.
8. You shall not steal.
9. You shall not lie.
10. Do not covet, but be content with what you have.

Affirmation: I will obey the Ten Commandments!

Balaam

The Israelites traveled on to the plain of Moab and camped near the Jordan River. The Moabites were frightened to see so many people. "What if they attack us?" they said. "We will be destroyed!" So the king of Moab sent messengers to find the prophet named Balaam. They asked Balaam to put a curse on the Israelites so the Moabites could defeat them in battle.

They called for Balaam!

Do Not Go With Them

Balaam said, "Spend the night here. I will ask God what He wants me to do." That night, the Lord spoke to Balaam, "Do not go with these men. You must never curse My people who are blessed." When he told the messengers that the Lord would not allow him to curse the Israelites, they said, "Don't let God stop you from doing this. We will pay you lots of money." Balaam was tempted by what they were offering and said, "I'll ask God again."

"I'll ask God again."

A Talking Donkey

The next day Balaam got up, saddled his donkey, and left with the messengers of Moab. God was very angry that Balaam had disobeyed. He sent an angel with a drawn sword to stand in the road to block the way. Balaam's donkey saw the angel and turned off the road into a field. Balaam beat his donkey for doing this. But he could not see the angel. This happened a second and third time until finally the Lord opened the donkey's mouth and she said to Balaam, "What have I done to you to make you beat me three times?"

The Lord opened Balaam's eyes.

Balaam couldn't believe his ears! "A talking donkey?" he thought. "You are acting crazy. If I had a sword I'd kill you right here!" Then the Lord opened Balaam's eyes and he saw the angel of the Lord standing in the road with his sword drawn. "Your donkey saw me and turned away from me three times. If she had not, I would have killed you, for you have disobeyed the Lord, and I am sent to stop you."

Balaam said to the angel, "I have sinned. I will turn around and go back." The angel said, "Go on with these men, but speak only what I tell you." Balaam agreed and went on with the messengers to meet with the king of Moab. Instead of cursing the God of Israel, he praised the Lord again and again for His goodness and faithfulness.

The king was furious. "Go! I told you to curse my enemies, not bless them." Then the prophet Balaam told the king that Moab would soon be defeated, and out of Israel would come a great ruler. The king went away very sad.

The King was furious.

Joshua's Shout

After Moses died, the Lord spoke to Joshua saying, "Get ready to cross the Jordan River. The promised land awaits you. I will walk with you, Joshua, as I did with Moses. I will make you a strong leader, so be courageous and obey My laws."

Joshua shouted to the people, "Get ready, for in three days we cross the Jordan River into the promised land!"

The Promised Land awaits you!

93

Two Spies

At that time there were people already living in Canaan. Joshua knew that he must defeat them if they were going to possess the land. Wisely, he sent two spies into the great walled city of Jericho. Soon, he would know their strength and if they were preparing for battle.

The two spies secretly crossed the Jordan and entered Jericho. They stayed with a woman named Rahab, but the king soon found out!

They entered Jericho.

Up on the Roof

He sent messengers to Rahab who said, "Bring out the two men who are spying on us. We know they're here!" Secretly, Rahab had hidden the two men on the roof of her house. "They were here, but they're gone. Perhaps you can catch them on the road if you hurry."

Just before nightfall, Rahab went back to the roof and said to the spies, "I have helped you, now you must help me. I know that the Lord is mighty and He has given this land to you."

"I know the Lord is mighty."

The River Miracle

"When the battle comes, save me and my family." The men agreed that if Rahab would not tell the king about them, they would save her family. Rahab's house was part of the great wall, so that night the men climbed out of Rahab's window, down a long rope and escaped into the hills. The spies returned to Joshua, "The Lord is surely giving our people this land. The Canaanites are afraid of us!"

Three days later, Joshua said to the people, "Tomorrow we cross the Jordan River. The ark of the Lord will go before you. Follow behind it, for great is our Lord!" Then came another miracle. As soon as the priests carrying the ark set foot in the rushing current of the Jordan River, the waters stopped flowing. The Israelites could then pass through the river on dry ground. God had made a way like He had done at the Red Sea! Not until the last person came out of the river did the waters flow again.

As Joshua neared the city of Jericho, he met a strange man with his sword drawn. Joshua went to him and said, "Are you for us or against us?"

"I command the invisible army of the Lord," he replied. Joshua fell face down with fear and respect. Then the Lord told Joshua what he must do to win the coming battle.

God had made a way.

The Day of Battle Comes

The day of the battle came. Seven priests blowing seven trumpets marched around the city of Jericho one time. The ark of the Lord was right behind them. An armed guard marched ahead of the priests and followed up behind the ark. They circled Jericho once and no one spoke a single word. "What are they doing?" cried the people of Jericho. "God is going to destroy us!"
They were afraid.

Seven priests blew seven trumpets.

Shout!

God commanded Joshua and his army to march around the city each day for six days. On the seventh day, the people marched around Jericho seven times. But the seventh time, just as the priests sounded the trumpet blast, Joshua commanded the nation, "Shout! For the Lord has given you the city! Shout! Shout!"

The people shouted
and the trumpets blasted, louder
and louder, until the walls of Jericho began to crack
and came tumbling down! The city was captured. Rahab
and her family who had helped them were saved.

"The Lord has given you the city."

Mighty Samson

When Joshua was 110 years old, he died. Joshua's life had pleased the Lord. But the children and grandchildren of the Israelites were doing things that did not please the Lord.

On a day when Israel had fallen into sin, the Lord allowed the Philistines to make them slaves.

Joshua had pleased the Lord.

Chosen to Serve

At the very same time the angel of the Lord appeared to an Israelite woman who was unable to have children and said, "You will soon have a little baby boy.

Therefore, do not drink any wine while you are pregnant.

When the baby is born, do not cut his hair, for he has been chosen to serve the Lord and deliver Israel from the Philistines."

A little baby boy named Samson was born. He grew to be very strong, and the Lord blessed him.

"Do not cut his hair."

Samson Betrayed

When Samson became a man, he fell in love with a woman named Delilah. She did not believe in God. The Philistine rulers went to her and said, "Find out what makes Samson so strong and we will give you lots of money." She agreed.

Delilah begged Samson to tell her the secret of his strength, but he would not. Three times she asked, but Samson would not tell her. Finally, he said, "My hair has never been cut, because I was set apart to God since birth. If my head were shaved, I would become as weak as any other man."

So Delilah went straight to the rulers and told them the secret of Samson's strength. That night while Samson slept, she let the Philistines in to shave his head. With his strength gone, Samson was blinded and put into prison. The people celebrated and shouted, "Bring out Samson that he may amuse us!"

They set Samson between the two support pillars of the temple. Now the temple was very crowded that day. Three thousand men and women were on the roof watching. Then Samson prayed.

Samson is bound between two pillars.

The Temple Falls!

"God, please remember me and strengthen me." Samson gave a mighty push on the pillars. They began to crack into pieces and suddenly, the whole temple fell killing Samson and all the people in it.

Affirmation: The Lord is my strength!

Suddenly the whole temple fell.

Ruth and Naomi

The judges were
ruling Israel in the
days when a terrible
famine came. A man named
Elimelech, his wife Naomi, and
their two sons left Bethlehem and moved
to Moab where there was plenty of food. While
in Moab, Elimelech died, leaving Naomi alone with two
sons. Sometime later, her sons married Moabite women
named Orpah and Ruth.

A terrible famine came.

Where You Go

They lived as a happy family for about ten years, and then both of her sons died. When Naomi learned that the famine in Judah had ended, she prepared to leave Moab and return home. Ruth and Orpah walked with Naomi part of the way because they loved her very much. Naomi said, "Each of you must go back to your mother's house. May the Lord show kindness to you."

Orpah returned home to her mother, but Ruth said, "Where you go I will go. Your people will be my people, and your God my God."

"Your people will be my people."

Ruth Works the Fields

So the two women traveled on to Bethlehem where the barley harvest had just begun. It was a custom in those days that the poor would follow behind the harvesters and pick up any barley left behind. It was called "gleaning."

"I will go to the fields and glean," Ruth told Naomi. Ruth began working in a field owned by a man named Boaz, a relative of Naomi's.

Ruth began working the fields.

Kind Boaz

Boaz noticed how hard Ruth was working and asked who she was. "She's a young woman from Moab who returned with Naomi," answered the foreman. Boaz liked Ruth and said, "Please stay close by and do not glean anywhere else. Stay near the other women and I'll make sure you are protected."

Ruth bowed and said, "Why are you being so kind to me?" Boaz replied, "I've heard how you left your home to care for Naomi. May the Lord bless you for what you have done."

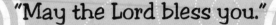

"May the Lord bless you."

A Baby is Born

Boaz helped Ruth in many ways. He made sure that she had enough to eat. He admired her very much because she always took care of Naomi. Boaz fell in love with Ruth and asked her to marry him. They were married one sunny day and soon a baby named Obed was born. He would be the father of Jesse who would be the father of David, the king of Israel. Naomi continued to live with Ruth and Boaz, and was very happy.

David and Goliath

Samuel was the last judge to rule Israel. The people of Israel decided they wanted a king, so Samuel chose Saul. Saul became the first king of Israel.

Israel met the Philistine army on the battlefield. Now the Philistines had a champion warrior named Goliath. Goliath stood over nine feet tall and carried a heavy javelin and spear. His armor was made of bronze and glistened in the sunlight. Who could defeat such a giant?

Who could defeat such a giant!

Goliath Mocks the Lord

One morning, Jesse, son of Obed, sent his youngest son David to the battlefield to deliver a meal to David's older brothers who were soldiers. When David arrived and heard Goliath mocking the Lord's army, he said to Saul, "Do not fear this Philistine. I will go and fight him!"

You? Fight the giant? Why, you are only a boy," scoffed Saul. "He is a mighty warrior, a killer. You are a shepherd boy. You cannot fight him."

"I will go and fight him."

Then David answered, "As I kept my father's sheep, I once fought a lion and rescued the sheep. When the lion turned on me, I killed it. This giant will be defeated, for the Lord who delivered me from the lion and the bear will deliver me from the hand of this Philistine." Saul said, "Go, and the Lord be with you."

"The Lord be with you."

Five Stones and a Slingshot

So he gathered his staff, five stones, and his slingshot and started walking directly toward Goliath.

When Goliath saw that Israel had sent a young boy to fight him, he grew angry. "Am I a dog that you come at me with a stick? Come here and I'll tear you apart!" Then David spoke, "You come against me with a sword and a spear, but I come against you in the name of the Lord Almighty, the God of Israel's army, whom you mock. This day you will die!"

"I'll tear you apart!"

Goliath was furious and moved in to attack. But David took out one of the stones and loaded it into his slingshot. With all the power of the Lord behind him, he let it go. Bam! It struck Goliath right in the forehead and sank deep.

David loaded a stone.

Goliath Defeated

Goliath staggered, his knees buckled, and he fell like a giant oak tree. Goliath was not dead, so David ran and stood over Goliath. Taking Goliath's own sword, he killed him.

The Lord had given Israel the battle. The Philistine army ran away, but Israel went after them and defeated them. From that day on, David remained in King Saul's service.

He fell like a giant oak tree!

Kindhearted King

During a fierce battle with the Philistine army, King Saul found his army outnumbered and fled. Saul and his three sons, including Jonathan, were all killed that day. David became the new king of Israel.

David did not know that Jonathan, his dearest friend, had a five-year-old son named Mephibosheth. In that day when a new king came to the throne, he would search for the children of the old king and have them sent away or killed so they could never be king. That is why Mephibosheth's nurse took the boy and fled for safety. In her haste, she stumbled and dropped the little boy, crippling him for life.

The nurse fled for safety.

One day, King David asked if any of Saul's family was alive. He wanted to show them kindness because of his promise to Jonathan. A former servant to Saul named Ziba told him Jonathan's crippled son Mephibosheth was indeed alive. David sent for him and he was brought to the palace. Mephibosheth must have thought David was going to kill him. He fell on his face and cried, "Here is your servant."

But David said, "Don't be afraid. I will give back to you all the land your grandfather Saul owned and you shall always be welcome at my dinner table." Because of David's kindness, Mephibosheth became a part of the king's family.

"You are always welcome!"

Abigail Was a Peacemaker

Abigail had a foolish husband named Nabal. He had insulted King David. This made King David so angry that he planned to kill Nabal. When Abigail heard about King David's plan, she took food and gifts to him to make peace for Nabal.

Even though Nabal was wrong, Abigail helped David to see that it would be wrong for him to kill Nabal. David's heart was changed. Abigail had brought peace to an angry king!

David's heart was changed.

Ahab and Jezebel's Firefall

Some years after Solomon died, Ahab became king of Israel. He was the most wicked kings to ever reign over Israel. He and his evil wife Jezebel led the Israelites in the worship of Baal, a false god. Now there appeared before Ahab a prophet named Elijah. Now there appeared before Ahab a prophet named Elijah. Elijah told Ahab, "Because of your great wickedness, it will not rain unless I say so."

"It will not rain unless I say so."

Meeting on Mount Carmel

Then the Lord sent Elijah eastward to hide. There he drank from a crystal clear brook, and the Lord ordered ravens to bring him bread and meat.

Elijah stayed hidden for three years, and just as he said it did not rain during this time. Then the Lord told Elijah to return to Ahab and he would send rain. When Ahab saw Elijah he said, "Is it really you, the big trouble-maker of Israel?" Elijah said, "Not I, but you and your family have caused Israel's trouble by worshiping Baal. Call for your priests and meet me on Mount Carmel."

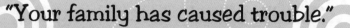

"Your family has caused trouble."

Answer with Fire!

When they were all gathered on the mountain, Elijah spoke. "Will you ever make up your mind? If the Lord Yahweh is God, follow him; but if Baal is God, follow him. I am the only prophet of Yahweh here today. There are 450 prophets of Baal here. Therefore, I challenge you.

Prepare two bulls for sacrifice and lay them on a bed of wood. All of you call on your god and I alone will call on mine. The one who answers with fire from heaven is the true god." They agreed to his challenge.

"I alone will call on the true God."

Elijah's God Is True

All day long the priests of Baal called on their false god, but nothing happened. Elijah laughed at them, "Shout louder, maybe he's gone on vacation." Finally, Elijah called to the people, "Come to me." They watched as Elijah built an altar with twelve stones. Then he had them pour twelve barrels of water on his firewood. Elijah called to the Lord, "Today, O Lord, let it be known that You are the one true God."

Instantly fire fell from heaven burning up the meat, the wood, even the stones. "Kill these false prophets," demanded Elijah. And it was done. Soon the skies darkened and the rain began to fall. Elijah's God was the one true God.

Affirmation: I will praise the Lord of heaven, the one true God.

Soon the skies darkened.

Elijah and the Chariot of Fire

Elijah and Elisha were traveling from city to city proclaiming the name of the Lord when God decided to take Elijah up to heaven. It seemed that everywhere they went, other prophets knew Elijah's earthly ministry was about to end. But Elisha asked them not to speak about it. Finally, Elijah, Elisha, and about 50 followers reached the banks of the Jordan River.

God decided to take Elijah to heaven.

A Double Measure

Elijah took off his coat, rolled it up, and struck the water with it. The waters of the Jordan parted to the left and right making a pathway to cross through. Only Elijah and Elisha walked across the river. "Can I give you any blessing before I leave you?" Elijah asked Elisha. Elisha answered, "Let me have your faith and love in a double measure."

Elijah sighed, "What you ask is very hard to do, but if you see me when I leave this earth, it will be yours."

"What you ask is hard!"

Up in a Whirlwind

As they were walking and talking together, suddenly a chariot of fire pulled by horses of fire appeared from the sky and drove between the two men. In an instant, Elijah went up into heaven in a whirlwind.

Elisha saw this and shouted, "My Father! My Father! The chariots and horsemen of Israel!" Then Elijah and the chariot were gone.

Elisha humbled himself before the Lord by tearing his clothes. He picked up Elijah's coat which had fallen and dipped it into the Jordan River. The waters parted again and Elisha crossed to join the other followers. They all bowed before Elisha, for they knew the Spirit of God was with him.

The water parted and Elisha crossed.

Josiah: A Teenager Finds a Treasure

When Josiah was eight years old, his father King Amon died making Josiah king. King Amon had disobeyed the Lord, as did his father King Manasseh. They worshiped idols, but Josiah loved the Lord God and sought to please him in every way. So, while he was still very young, he destroyed the idols that were in Judah. Then he sent workers to repair the temple of the Lord.

Josiah loved the Lord!

While the workers were cleaning the temple, they found
Israel's treasure. There in the dust was the Book of the
Law written by Moses. It had been lost for many years.
Shaphan, the scribe, took the scroll and ran to the palace.
There he read the law to young King Josiah. The law
warned Israel that if they disobeyed the commandments,
God would send great trouble upon them. Josiah asked God
for forgiveness for the way his people had sinned. He called
all the people of Israel together and read the law and
promised to obey it.

They promised to obey the law.

Mixed-Up Builders

The prophet Ezra tells the story of the Israelites' return from Babylon. Now free from slavery, King Cyrus ordered the temple to be rebuilt.

"Rebuild the temple!"

Ezra also had the king's blessing to choose judges and rulers who knew the laws of God. Ezra was to teach Israel how to live God's way. "Praise be to the Lord," said Ezra, "for a king who honors the Lord."

This made the Jews very happy. Everyone brought gold and silver and precious oils and ointments to be used in rebuilding the temple.

People who were already living in the land also came to help. These people worshiped the God of heaven and false gods at the same time. This displeased the Lord. So the Jews decided to rebuild the temple without the help of people who dishonored the Lord.

This made the people very angry, so they tried to stop the building. When King Cyrus died, armed men forced the work to stop. But God sent two prophets, Haggai and Zechariah, to encourage the people to start building again. "We can do it without the help of idol worshipers. Arise and build!" When the new king, Darius, blessed the Jews and allowed them to rebuild, it was an answer to prayer.

"We can do it!"

Nationwide Search

Once, in the city of Susa the capital of Persia, great king Xerxes gave a banquet in honor of his many governors. As the banquet went on, King Xerxes called for Vashti the queen. "Place the royal crown on Vashti's head and bring her to me," commanded the king, for she was very beautiful.

When Queen Vashti refused to come, the king was very angry. He sent Vashti away and ordered a nationwide search for a new queen.

Vashti refused to come.

Esther Becomes Queen

Now there was a Jewish man named Mordecai who also lived in Persia. He had a beautiful cousin named Esther. In obedience to the king's order, Esther was taken to the king's palace. Mordecai asked her to tell no one that she was Jewish.

When the king saw Esther, he loved her. He set the royal crown on her head and made her the new queen.

He set the royal crown on her head.

An Evil Plan

One day Mordecai was sitting at the king's gate waiting to see Esther. He heard two soldiers planning to kill the king. Mordecai told Esther, who in turn, told the king. "Mordecai has told me of a plot to kill you, my King!" said Esther. The king had the two men arrested and they were found guilty. Mordecai had saved the king's life and it was written down in the history books.

The King was saved!

I Bow to the Lord

After this, King Xerxes honored Haman by making him second in command of Persia. Haman was a very proud man and at the king's order everyone was to bow before him. But Mordecai would bow to no one except the Lord. This angered Haman. When he later found out that Mordecai was an Israelite, he began to look for a way to destroy them all. Then he came up with an evil plan.

Haman was very proud.

For Such a Time as This

Haman went to King Xerxes and said, "There are people in your kingdom who do not obey your laws, O King, but rather God's laws. This is not good for us. Therefore, let us send soldiers to kill them." The king agreed, so Haman sent out an order to kill the Jews.

When Mordecai heard about Haman's evil plan, he sent word to Esther. "Perhaps God has made you Queen of Persia for such a time as this. Maybe He will use you to save His people."

"There are people who obey God!"

Pray for Three Days

Then Esther sent word back to Mordecai. "Gather all the Jews in Susa and pray for three days. Though it is against the law for me to go to the king, I will do so. Pray that the king will have mercy and stop Haman's evil plan." Mordecai did as Esther asked.

On the third day, Esther prepared a banquet and only invited the king and Haman. "What can I do for you?" the king asked. "Name it and it will be done." Esther spoke, "Will you and Haman come tomorrow to another special banquet? Then I will tell you both."

Esther prepared a banquet.

Honor a Special Man

As Haman left, he again passed Mordecai at the gate. Again, Mordecai refused to bow. Haman in his anger decided to start building the place where Mordecai would be executed. That night, as the king was reading the history book, he discovered he had not honored Mordecai for saving his life. He called Haman and said, "I want to honor a special man. What should I do?"

Haman thought he was the man to be honored, so he said, "Let him wear the royal robe and be put on the king's horse and lead him through the city proclaiming, "The king is honoring this man!" So Haman was asked to honor Mordecai in the way. Haman was furious.

Haman thought he was the man.

To the Gallows!

Later, Haman and the king went to dine with Esther. "What is your request? Tell me and it shall be yours," said the king to Esther. "O King, spare me and the life of my people."

"Spare you? You are queen!" said the king. "Yes," said Esther, "but I am also a Jew. And there is a man in the kingdom who wants to kill all of the jews."

"Who is this man?" asked the king. "Haman," she replied. "He is an evil man."

The king was furious and that night Haman was hanged on the very gallows he had built for Mordecai. God's people were saved!

God's people were saved.

The Psalm of the Shepherd King David

The Lord is my shepherd, I shall not want.
He makes me to lie down in green pastures.
He leads me beside the still waters.
He restores my soul.
He leads me in the paths of
righteousness for His name's sake.
Yea though I walk through the valley
of the shadow of death,
I will fear no evil, for You are with me.
Your rod and Your staff, they comfort me.
You prepare a table before me in
the presence of my enemies.
You anoint my head with oil.
My cup runs over.
Surely goodness and mercy shall follow
me all the days of my life,
And I will dwell in the house of the Lord
Forever.

The Lord is my Shepherd!

Dry Bones

When Ezekiel the prophet arrived on the scene, the Israelite nation was held captive in Babylon. At the very same time Jeremiah was preaching near Jerusalem. God called Ezekiel to preach a message of hope. "God has not forgotten you!" he shouted. "God does not want anyone to die with sin in their lives. Repent!"

"God has not forgotten you!"

A Strange Dream

One night, God caused Ezekiel to have a strange dream. Ezekiel was taken to the middle of a large valley. This valley was full of bones. God walked with Ezekiel back and forth through the valley. There was no end to the old dry bones.

Then the Lord asked, "Can these bones live?"
Ezekiel answered, "I don't know, Lord. Only You know!"
Then the Lord spoke again, "Ezekiel, say to these bones 'You will live. The Lord will breathe life into you and you will come to life. Then you will know that I am the Lord.'"

"Can those bones live?"

Ezekial Obeys

"Dry bones can live!"

Ezekiel obeyed the Lord. As he was speaking, there came a rattling sound. The bones were coming back together. And as they came together, the Lord caused them to be covered with skin. But there was no breath in them yet. Then the Lord said, "Ezekiel, tell them the Lord God says to breathe!" As soon as Ezekiel spoke, breath entered their bodies and they came to life. They stood up on their feet, a vast army.

Then the Lord spoke again. "Ezekiel, here's what this vision means: My people think there is no hope. They believe they are cut off from me and dead just like those dry bones. Tell them that the Lord is going to bring them back to life and return them once again to the promised land."

Ezekiel proclaimed the message, "Dry bones can live. All things are possible with God."

Daniel in the Lion's Den

In the third year of the reign of King Jehoiakim, Jerusalem was attacked and defeated by King Nebuchadnezzar of Babylon. The Babylonians carried off the cups and other vessels from the holy temple. They began using them in their own idol worship. The king then ordered the smartest and most handsome young men of Israel to be brought to his palace. There they would stay for three years being trained to serve the king. One of these young men was a Jewish boy named Daniel.

The smartest would serve the King.

Water and Vegetables

Each day Daniel was given a portion of royal food and wine, but he refused to eat it. He chose instead to eat vegetables and drink water. In doing so, he did not break the Jewish law.

When the three years of training ended, all of the young men were presented to King Nebuchadnezzar. Daniel was by far the smartest and most handsome of them all. That day, he entered the king's service. He served for many years until Nebuchadnezzar died and his grandson Belshazzar became king.

Daniel was the smartest of them all.

The Mysterious Hand

The Lord gave Daniel the gift of interpreting dreams.
On many occasions, Daniel was able to interpret the
king's dreams and he soon became well-known as a
very wise man of God. One night, Belshazzar gave a
great party. A thousand guests were there. The king
gave orders to bring out the gold and silver cups his
father had stolen from the Jewish temple years ago.
They began pouring wine into these holy cups while
they praised their false gods. The Lord was very
angry. Suddenly, a mysterious hand appeared in the
room and began writing strange words on the palace
wall.

The king collapsed with fear. He called out, "If anyone
can tell me what this means, speak now and I will
make you third in command of Babylon." All of the
king's wise men tried, but they could not read the
message. Then the queen spoke, "There is a man who
walks with the God of Israel in your kingdom. His
name is Daniel. Call for him. He will tell you what
the writing means."

So Daniel was brought before the king. "Can you read
this? Tell me!" demanded the king. "Yes, O king. God
has given me the ability to read it," answered Daniel.
"It says you have not honored the living God, but
mocked Him."

"You have not honored God."

Daniel Becomes a President

Daniel was made third in command of Babylon. But that night Belshazzar, king of Babylon was killed and Darius the Mede took over the kingdom.

King Darius hand-picked 120 princes to rule his new kingdom. He then selected three presidents to oversee the princes. Of these three, Daniel became the most important. The other presidents and governors were jealous that Daniel had been honored in this way, so they plotted against him.

Others plotted against Daniel.

A New Law

They went to the king as a group and said, "O King Darius, all of us have agreed that you should make a new law this day; a law that will unite the kingdom. The new law would make it a crime for anyone to pray to any god or man but you, O King, for the next thirty days. And if anyone should break the new law, they would be thrown into the lions' den." So King Darius agreed and it was put into writing.

Now when Daniel heard about the new law, he went upstairs to his room, got down on his knees, and prayed, just as he had done before. When the princes and governors found Daniel praying, they ran to the king and said, "Daniel has broken your new law, O King. He must be punished. Throw him to the lions!" Darius did not want to harm Daniel, but these evil men had tricked him. So King Darius gave the order, "Put Daniel into the lions' den."

They took Daniel to the lions' den and threw him in. Then King Darius spoke to Daniel, "May the God whom you serve rescue you!" Then they sealed the den shut and the king returned to the palace.

At dawn, the king arose from a sleepless night and hurried to the den. "Daniel," he cried, "are you alive? Has your God rescued you from the lions?" Daniel answered, "My God has sent an angel who shut the mouths of the lions. They have not hurt me, nor have I done any wrong to you, O King."

"Throw him to the lions."

A God Who Saves

"Pull him up!" shouted the king. Then, at the king's command, those men who had falsely accused Daniel were thrown into the den of lions. Then King Darius sent a letter throughout the kingdom which read: All the people of the kingdom must fear and respect the God of Daniel, for He is the living God who rescued and saved Daniel from the lions.

Daniel loved the Lord and faithfully served Him.

Affirmation: I will honor the living God!

A Whale of a Tale

One day the Lord spoke to Jonah the prophet. "Go to Nineveh and tell them that they must stop sinning." But Jonah didn't want to go.

He boarded a sailing ship bound for Tarshish. But the Lord knew Jonah had disobeyed His command, so He sent a violent storm over the sea.

Jonah didn't want to go!

He boarded a ship to Tarshish.

Prayer Meeting in a Boat!

The sailors were so afraid, they began to pray to their false gods. They even began to throw the ship's cargo into the sea to make it float better. The other sailors began to think that Jonah was somehow responsible for the storm.

So they asked him, "Is it your fault we are in this terrible trouble? Who are you? Where are you from?" Jonah answered, "I am a Hebrew. I worship the Lord of heaven who made the sea."

"Throw the cargo in the sea!"

Swallowed by a Fish

What can we do to calm the raging sea?" the sailors cried.
"Throw me into the sea and it will become calm!" Jonah said.
"Forgive us, Lord," the men prayed. Then they picked Jonah
up and threw him into the raging sea.

There he stayed for three days.

Suddenly, the sea was calm. Everything was still. When this happened, all of the sailors made promises to serve the God of Jonah. But poor Jonah was sinking deeper and deeper below the waves until a great fish swallowed Jonah whole. There he stayed for three days.

When Jonah realized what had happened, he began to pray, "I am in deep trouble, O Lord, and yet You have saved my life. Hear my song of thanksgiving!"

Better to Obey the First Time

As Jonah continued to pray, the giant fish was swimming toward dry land, where it spit Jonah out. The Lord spoke to Jonah for the second time: "Go to Nineveh and proclaim My message of salvation." This time, Jonah went straight to Nineveh!

For three days Jonah told everyone in Nineveh, "Repent, or God will destroy this city in forty days!" When the people heard Jonah's voice, they knew he was preaching the truth. All of Nineveh believed God and declared a city-wide day of prayer and fasting. They turned from their evil ways and blessed the God of Jonah.

They blessed the God of Jonah.

Habakkuk's Joy Was in the Lord

The prophet Habakkuk was joyful! He knew the secret of lasting happiness. It was not found in things you make or buy. Habakkuk knew that real joy and happiness comes from loving and trusting the Lord.

Habakkuk said that we should rejoice even if the fig tree does not bloom. We should be happy even if there are no grapes on the vine, no sheep in the pasture, or cattle in the stalls. We should rejoice because God is our God.

"Rejoice, for God is our God!"

New Testament

Gabriel's Visit

Now this is how the birth of Jesus Christ came about. In the days when Herod was king of Judea, there lived a priest named Zacharias. He had a wonderful wife named Elizabeth. They had grown old together but had no children.

There lived a priest named Zacharias.

A Message from God

One day Zacharias was in the temple preparing an offering to the Lord when suddenly, an angel appeared before him.

Zacharias was afraid! "Do not be afraid, for God has heard your prayers. Soon you and Elizabeth will have a baby boy. You are to name him John, for he will be a great man of God. Because of his preaching many will repent and turn back to God. He will prepare the way for the coming of the Lord."

Zacharias said to the angel, "How can this be true? I am too old to have children and so is my wife."

The angel said, "Do not fear!"

A Silent Zacharias

"I am Gabriel, a messenger sent by God to tell you this wonderful news. But since you have not believed me, you shall be unable to speak until all of these things have happened." Then as quickly as he had come, Gabriel disappeared.

Outside the temple, the people were waiting for Zacharias wondering what was keeping him. Finally, he came out unable to speak. He used sign language to try to tell them what had happened. They thought he had seen a vision!

He came out unable to speak!

A Message for Mary

Finally, a silent Zacharias returned home. Soon Elizabeth discovered that she was going to have a baby, just as Gabriel had said.

Now sometime later, Gabriel was sent by God to the city of Nazareth to visit a young woman named Mary. She was engaged to marry a carpenter named Joseph.

But before their wedding day, Gabriel came to her and said, "Hello favored one, the Lord is with you!" Mary had never heard such a greeting before and wondered, "What does it mean?"

"The Lord is with you!"

Gabriel spoke again, "Do not be afraid Mary, for I have a message for you from the Lord. You are going to have a baby boy and you shall call His name Jesus. He will be great and will be called the Son of God, and His kingdom will have no end!"

Mary was confused. "How can this be?" she asked. "I have no husband yet."

"You shall call His name Jesus!"

Gabriel answered, "Nothing is impossible with God. Even Elizabeth your relative is going to have a baby, though she is very old. For nothing will be impossible with God."

"I am the servant of the Lord," said Mary. "Let all that you have said be done in my life." And in an instant, the angel was gone.

"Nothing will be impossible with God!"

The Baby Jumps!

Mary couldn't wait to tell Elizabeth about Gabriel's visit. She left Nazareth at once and hurried through the hills of Judah. When she arrived at Zacharias' house, she hurried inside and called, "Elizabeth! It is me, Mary." When Elizabeth heard Mary's voice, her baby jumped inside her and the Spirit of God filled her. "How blessed you are, Mary, to be the mother of my Lord."

The Spirit of God filled her!

Mary wondered. "How could Elizabeth know about the baby Jesus? I haven't told her yet. I am happy," said Mary, "because God is my Lord and Savior. Holy is His name." Mary stayed with Elizabeth for three months and then she returned home.

Affirmation: Nothing is impossible with God!

"God is my Lord and Savior."

John is Born

Time passed and soon Elizabeth's baby was born. Their friends and church leaders wanted to name the child Zacharias, like his father. But Elizabeth said, "No, his name will be John."

"You can't call him John," they said. "Let's ask Zacharias what the child's name will be." On a tablet Zacharias wrote, "His name is John." At that very moment, Zacharias could once again speak. And oh, how he praised the Lord! "This must be a very special child," the people said, "for the hand of the Lord is upon him."

"His name is John!"

Joseph's Dream

When Mary told Joseph all of the things that had happened to her and Elizabeth, he was very confused. But one night as he slept, an angel of the Lord appeared to him in a dream and said, "Mary is a good woman. Do not put her away. Take her as your wife, for her baby is a miracle baby that God himself has given her."

"Her baby is a miracle baby!"

Wedding Bells for Mary

"And you shall call His name Jesus, for He will save His people from their sins."

When Joseph awoke from his dream, he did exactly what the angel asked him to do. He took Mary as his wife and he never doubted again.

He never doubted again.

Journey to Bethlehem

Now it came about that the Roman king, Caesar Augustus, wanted to know how many people were living in his kingdom. So everyone, including Joseph and Mary, had to return to their own city to be counted. Mary was ready to have her baby, but still they made the journey from Nazareth to the city of David which is called Bethlehem.

Mary was ready to have her baby.

Lay Him in a Manger

When they arrived in Bethlehem, it was very crowded. Mary was ready to give birth, and though Joseph looked everywhere for a room, there was none to be found. Finally, Joseph and Mary came to a stable where sheep and livestock were kept. There Jesus Christ, the Son of God, was born. And Mary wrapped Him in swaddling clothes and laid Him in a manger, which is a feeding box. There, under the stars of Bethlehem, the baby Jesus slept.

Wrapped Him in swaddling clothes.

The Shepherds Came

Nearby, there was a group of shepherds keeping watch over their flocks of sheep.

Suddenly, an angel of the Lord
appeared before them and the darkness was filled with
light! The shepherds were so afraid!

Then the angel spoke. "Do not be afraid, for I bring you
good news of a great joy! Today in Bethlehem, your Savior
is born who is Christ the Lord."

"Today in Bethlehem, your Savior is born!"

The Angels Sing

"Come and see the Lord! You will know it is He when you find the baby wrapped in swaddling clothes and lying in a manger."

Then suddenly, many angels appeared before them, praising God and saying, "Glory to God in the highest. And on earth, peace among men with whom He is pleased."

"Glory to God in the Highest"

When the angels departed, the shepherds said, "Let's go to Bethlehem right now to see this thing that has happened." So they hurried into town and found their way to Mary and Joseph. And just as the angel had said, they found Christ the Lord lying in a manger.

Now when they had seen all this, they told everyone about Jesus and the appearance of angels. The shepherds went back to their flocks, praising God all the way!

Affirmation: I love Jesus!

They found Jesus in a manger.

The Baptism of Jesus

Zacharias and Elizabeth's baby boy grew to be a very rugged man. He became known as John the Baptist and he lived and preached in the desert. For food he ate locusts and wild honey, and he wore a coat of camel hair.

His message was very simple, "Repent! Stop doing evil things and return to God's ways, for the kingdom of heaven is coming soon."

"Return to God's ways!"

Jesus is Baptized

Many people would come to John and be baptized in the Jordan River. They would tell God how sorry they were for not obeying Him and promised to live for Him.

Then one day as John stood in the Jordan River, he saw Jesus walking towards him to be baptized. John knew that Jesus had never sinned and did not need to be baptized. So John said, "It is I who needs to be baptized by You. Why do You come to me?"

Jesus replied, "It is important that you baptize Me now. By doing this, we show others the right thing to do."

When Jesus came up out of the water, the heavens opened, and the Spirit of God came down upon Him like a dove. Then a voice came from heaven saying, "This is My son. I love Him and I am very pleased with Him."

"This is My son. I love Him."

The Beatitudes

Jesus began His ministry near the Sea of Galilee. There He began telling everyone the good news of God's coming kingdom. He healed every kind of disease and sickness. The people loved Jesus. Every day the crowds grew bigger and bigger, so Jesus went up on a mountainside where there was plenty of room for everyone to gather. There He sat down and began to teach the people.

The people loved Jesus!

"Blessed are the poor in spirit, for theirs is the kingdom of heaven. Blessed are the ones who mourn, for they will be comforted. Blessed are the meek, for they will inherit the earth. Blessed are the pure in heart, for they will see God. Blessed are the peacemakers, for they will be the sons of God."

Jesus went on to say that we are to be happy when people say unkind or untrue things about us. "Rejoice and be happy," He said, "because you will have a great reward one day in the kingdom of heaven."

Affirmation: I will be happy in Jesus!

"Blessed are the poor in spirit."

Salt and Light

Jesus said that we are the salt of the earth, and real salt always makes people very thirsty. And when you're thirsty, you want a drink of water. Jesus told the people that we're supposed to be very salty and cause people who see us and hear us to want to know more about Jesus; to make them thirsty for God's Word. He said that if we lose our saltiness, we can't make people thirsty.

"Make them thirsty for God!"

You Are the Light of the World

Jesus also said, "You are the light of the world." When people walk in the light, they can see all the dangerous things that might have hurt them if they stumbled in the darkness. God's Word is like a light. So when we share our light and tell others about Jesus, we brighten their lives. We help them see Satan's stumbling blocks.

But if we hide our lights under a bowl and tell no one that Jesus lives in our hearts, our friends and family may never see Jesus, and fall down in the darkness.

Be a light!

Affirmation: I will be a light!

The Lord's Prayer

Matthew was a disciple of Jesus. As they traveled together, he would write down what Jesus taught. Matthew writes: "Jesus said that there is a right way to pray and a wrong way to pray. We should not say our prayers in front of people just to make them think we're good. This is a wrong reason to pray.

When we pray, we should go into our room, close the door, and pray to our heavenly Father in secret. God promises to answer this kind of prayer by rewarding us openly. Jesus said, when you pray, use this example:

"Pray to your Heavenly Father."

"Our Father, which art in heaven
Hallowed be Thy name.
Thy kingdom come, Thy will be done

on earth as it is in heaven.
Give us this day our daily bread.
Forgive us our debts as we forgive
our debtors. And lead us not
into temptation, but deliver
us from evil. For Thine is the
kingdom, the power and the
glory forever and ever."

God promises to answer!

Do Not Worry

"Look at the birds flying through the air," Jesus said. "They do not plant gardens to get food, nor do they pick corn or gather the seeds they eat. Yet, your Heavenly Father feeds them. So do not worry about what you will eat and drink," he said. "for you are much more precious in God's sight than these birds. God will provide what you need."

Jesus went on to say, "And why do you worry about your clothes? Look at the lilies growing wild in the fields. They do not make their own clothing, yet they are dressed as splendidly as a king. Our God has provided clothing for flowers; don't you think He will provide clothing for you? Have faith! Do not worry."

"Look at the birds!"

Do Not Judge Others

God does not want us to judge another person's actions. That will be His job. Rather, He wants us to be concerned about our own actions. That's why Jesus said, "Do not judge others, or you too will be judged. And in the very same way you judge others, you will be judged."

Each of us has done things that were not pleasing to God. In God's eyes, we are all sinners. Jesus said, "Before you tell your neighbor about a speck of sawdust in his eye, first take the plank out of your own eye. Then you will see things more clearly."

"Take the plank out of your own eye."

Ask, Seek, and Knock

Matthew writes concerning prayer, "Sometimes it takes a little time for prayers to be answered. But Jesus taught the people that they should never stop praying. Keep asking in prayer, and it will be given to you; keep seeking, and you will find what you are looking for; keep knocking, and the door will be opened for you! For God always hears our prayers. And He will answer; sometimes yes, sometimes no, sometimes wait."

"Never stop praying!"

"If you were a father and your child asked for bread, would you give him a stone? Or if your child asked for a fish, would you give him a snake? If we know how to give good gifts to our children, think of how much our Heavenly Father will give good gifts to those that ask Him! Treat others like you would want them to treat you: this is the golden rule!"

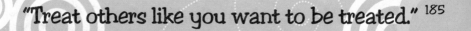

"Treat others like you want to be treated." ¹⁸⁵

The Wise and Foolish Builders

Jesus said that everyone who hears the word of God and does what it says is like a wise man who built his house upon a rock. Our "house" is our life and "the rock" is God's Word! When we build our lives on the solid rock of God's Word, we will stand! When the rains of trouble come, we will stand! When the streams of sickness rise, we will stand! When the winds of change come and beat against our house, it will not fall down! Because it is built on the solid rock of God's Word!

Now when Jesus finished His teaching, the crowd was amazed because He knew everything about the kingdom of God.

Affirmation: I will build my life on God's Word!

"We stand on God's Word."

The Call of the Disciples

Mark was a friend of Peter's who wrote down some of the stories Peter told about Jesus. One day as Jesus was walking beside the Sea of Galilee, He saw Peter and Peter's brother, Andrew. They were fishermen. "Come follow Me," Jesus said, "and I will make you fishers of men." At once they left their fishing nets and followed Him.

When they had gone a little further, they met James and his brother John who were also fishermen. As they were fixing their nets, Jesus said, "Come follow Me."

Without delay, they left their boat and followed Jesus.

They followed Jesus!

The Twelve

Sometime later, Jesus had called twelve men to be his disciples. They would spend time with him and learn God's Word. Then someday they would go out and preach the good news! They were Peter, Andrew, James, John, Philip, Bartholomew, Matthew, Thomas, another James, Thaddaeus, Simon, and Judas.

Simon

John

Thomas

James

Thaddaeus

Philip

Judas

Matthew

James Too!

Bartholomew

Andrew

Peter

They would preach the good news.

Rooftop Miracle

One day, Jesus was teaching in a home in Capernaum. The crowd grew so big that there was no room to stand inside. Even the doorways were jammed with people.

Some men came to see Jesus that day. They brought their friend who was sick and could not move. They believed that Jesus would heal him. "This crowd is too big," they said. "How will our friend ever see Jesus?" Then they had an idea!

"The crowd is too big!"

Great Faith in a Hole

The four men carried their friend, who lay on a mat, up to the roof. They began tearing away the rooftop to make a large hole right above Jesus! Then they lowered their friend down through the hole and he came to rest right in front of the Lord. Jesus knew these men must have great faith to do such a thing. So He said to the sick man, "Your sins are forgiven. Get up, take your mat, and go home."

"Get up and go home well!"

One Miracle Moment

Suddenly the man felt strength coming back into his arms and legs. He raised up ... he could move! Then he leaped off the mat and walked right through the crowd praising God!

Jesus had taken away his sickness and his sin, all in one miracle moment! This amazed everyone and they praised God, giving thanks saying, "We have never seen anything like this."

He leaped off the mat.

Jesus Calms the Storm

Mark tells us of another miracle Jesus did. "On another day, Jesus was teaching the people by a lake. Once again the crowds grew so big that Jesus had to get into a boat and float away from the shore. Then everyone could hear Him. There He sat and taught the people many lessons of faith."

Suddenly a storm came up.

When evening came, Jesus was very tired. "Let's go over to the other side of the lake," He said. So they left the crowds behind and set sail across the lake. Jesus went to sleep on a cushion in the back of the sailboat. Suddenly, a terrible storm came up. The waves began to break over the sides of the boat, tossing it back and forth.

Jesus went to sleep in the storm.

The disciples were frightened. They thought they might die, so they turned to Jesus. "Teacher!" they shouted. "Don't You care if we drown? Help us!" Jesus got up, faced the wind and the waves and shouted, "Quiet! Be still!" And at His word, the wind stopped blowing and the waters were calm.

Then Jesus said to His disciples, "Why were you so frightened? Where is your faith?" The disciples thought, "Who is this man? Even the wind and waves obey Him!"

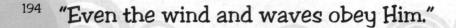

"Even the wind and waves obey Him."

Five Loaves and Two Fish

The news of Jesus' miracles began to spread all over the land. People came to Jesus from everywhere bringing Him their hurts and sickness; and Jesus loved them ... every one!

But now He needed some rest. "Let us go to a quiet place," said Jesus. So they set sail across the lake. As they sailed away, the people ran around the lake and were waiting for them when they reached the other side.

"Let us go to a quiet place."

When Jesus saw them, He loved them. They were like sheep without a shepherd; and after all, He was the Great Shepherd! So once again, He began teaching them and taking care of them.

It was late when the disciples said, "Jesus, send the people away so they can eat." But to their surprise He said, "You feed them."

"You feed them!"

"Feed them!" exclaimed the disciples. "That would cost too much!" Then Andrew spoke up. "There is a boy here with five loaves of bread and two fish. But how far will that go among so many?"

Then Jesus said to tell the people to sit down on the grass. As they were sitting down, Jesus took the five loaves and two fish and looked up into heaven. He thanked God and then began to break the loaves and fish into pieces.

Jesus broke the loaves and fish.

Five Thousand Fed!

Five thousand people were fed that day, and they all left with their bellies full. The disciples picked up twelve baskets full of bread and fish left behind by the crowd. Jesus has the power to supply all of our needs, no matter what!

Jesus has the power to supply our needs.

Mary and Martha

Mary and Martha were sisters. Though they both loved Jesus, they were very different. Martha was a doer. She prepared meals and cared for her home. Mary was a learner. She chose to listen and learn about her God.

One day Jesus came to visit. Martha, the doer, stayed busy. Mary, the learner, sat and listened to Jesus. Martha was upset that she wasn't helping. Martha burst into the room and demanded that Mary help. Jesus taught Martha that it is good to work, but it's better to learn about God.

Mary listened, while Martha worked.

Footprints on the Water

Jesus asked the disciples to sail ahead to Bethsaida while He said goodbye to the crowds. After they had gone, He went into the hills alone to pray.

When evening came, a mighty wind blew across the lake. The disciples could hardly row. Mark writes, "Jesus saw their trouble and went out to them, walking on the water!"

Jesus saw their trouble.

Peter's Great Faith

When they saw something coming toward them, they thought it was a ghost. They were very frightened! Then Jesus shouted, "It is I ... don't be afraid!" Peter said, "Lord, if it's You, tell me to come to You on the water." Jesus commanded, "Come."

Peter stepped out of the boat and walked to Jesus. But the mighty wind and the waves caused him to be afraid and lose faith. Then he began to sink. "Lord save me!" cried Peter.

Peter stepped out of the boat.

Jesus reached out His hand and caught Peter. "Why did you doubt?" asked Jesus. Then they both climbed into the boat.

All the men worshiped Jesus saying, "Truly You are the Son of God!"

"Truly You are the Son of God!"

Blind Bartimaeus

Bartimaeus was blind. As he sat begging by the roadside, he heard Jesus passing by. He cried out above the crowd, "Jesus! Have mercy!" He shouted louder until the people took him to Jesus. Then Jesus asked, "What do you want me to do for you?"

Bartimaeus believed that all things were possible with Jesus, even the healing of his blind eyes. With great faith Bartimaeus said, "Lord, heal me!" What joy filled his heart when Jesus said, "Receive your sight. Your faith has healed you!"

"Your faith has healed you!"

The Parable of the Sower

Once while a large crowd was gathering to see Jesus, He told this parable: "A farmer went out to plant his seeds. He took a handful and tossed them onto

A farmer went out to plant.

"Some landed on the pathway to be stepped on and eaten by birds. Some landed upon the rocks, but before they could grow strong, they withered because their roots had no rich earth beneath them.

Other seeds fell among the thorns and were choked as they began to grow. But some of the seeds fell into the moist, rich earth and they grew healthy and strong. At harvest time, there were many crops; a hundred times more than the farmer sowed."

Some seeds fell into the rich earth.

Then Jesus explained the meaning of the parable. "The seed is the Word of God. And like the seeds that fell along the pathway, some people hear the Word and receive it, but then the devil comes and confuses them and they no longer pay attention to God's Word. Because of this, they cannot be saved. And like the seeds that fell on the rocks, some people hear the Word of God and receive it with great joy. But then, when a time of trouble comes, they quickly fall away. This is because they have no deep roots of faith."

"The seeds that fall into the thorns are people who hear the Word of God and want to receive it, but their worries and cares of this life choke it out and they do not grow in faith.

But some seeds fall into good soil and bear much fruit in God's kingdom. These are people who hear the Word of God. They memorize it, and work very hard to produce a good crop for the Lord."

"Bear much fruit for the Lord!"

The Good Samaritan

Once a lawyer asked Jesus this tricky question, "If we are to love our neighbor as ourselves, who then is our neighbor?" Jesus answered, "A man was traveling from Jerusalem to Jericho when he was attacked by robbers. They took everything he had. They beat him up and left him by the roadside nearly dead. Soon, a priest came along. But when he saw the man, he passed by on the other side of the road.

"Who then is my neighbor?"

Another church worker came along. But seeing the man, he too, passed him by without helping him. But then came a Samaritan. He was from another country. But when he saw the man hurt and bleeding, he stopped and helped him. He bandaged his wounds, put him on his own donkey and took him to an inn. There he cared for the man.

He stopped and helped!

The next day, he took two silver coins and gave them to the innkeeper. The Samaritan said, 'Take care of this man and if you spend more than this, I will repay you.'"

Then Jesus said to the lawyer, "Which one of the three men was a good neighbor?" The lawyer answered, "Why, the one who helped him!" "Go and do likewise," Jesus told him.

"Go and do likewise."

The Mustard Seed

Jesus once explained what the kingdom of God was like. Luke records Jesus' words. Jesus said, "The kingdom of God is like a tiny little mustard seed which a farmer planted in his garden. When it received the rain and rich soil, it grew and became a great tree; strong enough for birds to sit in its branches."

God's kingdom is like a mustard seed. 211

The kingdom of God is in our hearts. It starts with just a little love and just a little faith. But then, as God helps us, we grow stronger and taller as believers!

"Grow strong and tall as believers"

Only One Said, "Thank You"

Leprosy is a very painful disease of the skin. Those who had this sickness were not allowed to come near healthy people. In fact, before they were allowed to come into the city, they had to show the priest they no longer had the disease.

There was a group of ten men who were sick with leprosy. When they saw Jesus, they called to him. "Have pity on us!" Jesus saw their disease and had pity. He said, "Go show yourselves to the priest." They obeyed. Soon they were healed, and they were so happy! But only one of the men turned back to say thank you to Jesus. Jesus was pleased with his thankfulness and faith.

Jesus was pleased with his faith.

One Lost Sheep

The church leaders in Jesus' day began to say bad things about Him because He invited tax collectors and sinners to eat with him. So Jesus told this parable to show them that God loves everyone.

"What if you had a hundred sheep and one was lost? Wouldn't you leave the ninety-nine sheep in the meadow and look until you found the lost one?"

"What if you lost one sheep?"

"And when you found him, wouldn't you be happy and carry the little lamb home on your shoulders? Then you'd call your friends together and say, 'Come celebrate with me for I have found my lost sheep!'

In the very same way, there is more celebration in heaven when one sinner comes to the Lord than over ninety-nine who do not need to repent. God is looking for lost sinners."

"Come celebrate with me!"

The Prodigal Son

Jesus told this parable to His disciples. There once lived a man who had two sons. One day, the younger son came to his father and said, "Father, I would like my share of your property now." For he was to receive half when his father died. His father gave him his share.

"Father, I would like my share."

The son then took the money and all that he owned and traveled to a far away country. There, he spent all his money having a good time and doing things his father had taught him not to do.

Then a terrible famine swept across the country and the boy had no money for food. He was very hungry!

He was very hungry.

TIme for a Change

To stay alive he took a job feeding pigs. He got so hungry, he would have eaten the pig food if someone had offered it to him. "My father's workers have plenty to eat," he thought. "I'll go back home and say, 'Father, I have disobeyed God and I have disobeyed you. I am not worthy to be called your son. But please, I only ask that you make me one of your workers.'" He left for home with a broken heart.

"My father's workers have plenty."

A Father's Love

While the boy was still far from the house, his father saw him coming. His heart was filled with love and mercy. He ran as fast as he could. "My son ... my son has come home!" he shouted.

He threw his arms around the boy and kissed him. "Father, I have disobeyed God and I have disobeyed you. I am no longer worthy to be called your son," said the boy.

"My son has come home."

But his father replied, "Quickly, bring me our finest robe and put it on my son. Put a ring on his finger and new shoes on his feet. Let us prepare the biggest meal ever and celebrate. For my son who I thought was dead is alive; he was lost, but now is found!"

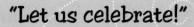

"Let us celebrate!"

An Angry Brother

Meanwhile, the older brother had come in from working in the fields. When he heard the music and dancing he asked, "What's all this celebration?"

A servant replied, "Your brother has come home and your father is preparing a big meal!" This angered the older brother, and he refused to go into the house.

His brother refused to go inside.

His father came outside and pleaded with him, but his son answered, "For years I have worked for you and done everything you have asked. Yet you never honored me in any way or celebrated my loyalty. But when this son of yours comes home after wasting all that you gave him, you have a celebration. It's not fair!"

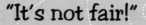

"It's not fair!"

"My son," said his father, "you are always with me. I love you and think of you always. Everything that I have is yours. But we must celebrate the homecoming of your brother ... for the son I thought to be dead is alive; he was lost, but now is found!"

This parable taught us that it is never too late to come back to God, for He always loves you!

It's never too late to come home to God.

The Promises of Jesus

The book of John was written by one of Jesus' disciples, John. John tells us, "In the very beginning when God was creating the heavens and the earth, Jesus was there with Him. Together, they created Adam and Eve, all the birds and animals, and this world we live in."

"Then 2,000 years ago, this same Jesus came into our world as a baby and grew to be the God/man who died for our sins." Jesus gives some wonderful promises to live by in the book of John.

Jesus gave some wonderful promises.

He Promises to Love Us

John writes; Jesus taught His followers many lessons about love. We are to love our neighbor as ourself. We are to love God and Jesus promises to love us! He said, "Anyone who loves Me will be loved by My Heavenly Father and I will show them love too!" How do we show Jesus we love Him? Jesus said, "If anyone loves Me, they will obey My teachings."

"Obey My teachings."

225

He Promises to Guide Us

One day Thomas, a disciple of Jesus, asked Him a very important question. "Lord, how can we know which way to go?" Jesus answered, "I am the Way and the Truth and the Life. No one comes to our Heavenly Father without first finding forgiveness in Me." If we follow the teachings of Jesus found in the Bible and pray, we will be on the right path!

Jesus said, "I am the Way."

He Promises to Protect Us

John writes; Jesus once said that we are like sheep and He was the Good Shepherd. Sheep do not know which way to go, so they listen for the Good Shepherd's voice and follow. Sheep never follow a stranger's voice; in fact, they run away from strangers. Jesus said, "I am the Good Shepherd, and the good shepherd is ready to die protecting His sheep." Jesus loves you and He will take care of you!

Jesus said, "I am the Good Shepherd." 227

He Promises to Comfort Us

Jesus said, "Do not let your hearts be troubled. Don't be filled with sorrow and sadness. Trust in God, for He is able to comfort you. Trust also in Me, for you have so much to look forward to! Keep your eyes fixed on heaven, for I'm going there to prepare a place just for you."

"Trust in God, trust also in Me."

He Promises to Send the Holy Spirit

Jesus said that if we love Him, we will obey His commandments. He said, "I will ask My Heavenly Father, and He will send the Holy Spirit to those who love God. He will walk with you and guide you each and every day, and He will teach you all things and will remind you of everything I have said to you."

He will send the Holy Spirit.

He Promises to Answer Prayer

Jesus taught His followers to pray. Prayer is talking to God. And since God is our dearest and closest friend, we should talk to Him every day.

Does God answer our prayers? Jesus said, "I tell you the truth, My Heavenly Father will give you whatever you ask for in prayer if you ask in My name." This means we should pray for things that would please Jesus.

Ask in Jesus' name.

He Promises Us Eternal Life

How long do most people live? Some live to be 70 years old, some 80, a few even 100 years old. The greatest promise of all in the Bible is the one Jesus made in John 3:16.

"For God so loved the world (that means you and me) that He gave His only begotten Son (that's Jesus!) that whosoever believes in Him should not perish (that means they will never die), but have everlasting life." If we love God, someday we will live with Jesus in heaven forever!

Someday all believers will live with Jesus! 231

Journey to the Cross

The feast of the Passover was only a few short days away. Jesus called His disciples together and said, "We are going to Jerusalem. There, all the things written about Me by the prophets will happen. I will be handed over to Roman leaders. I will be unkindly treated, and there I will die. But three days later I will come back to life again."

"Things written about Me will happen."

The Centurion Had Amazing Faith

A centurion is a Roman captain who has authority over 100 soldiers. There was once a centurion who asked Jesus to heal his servant who was ill. Jesus said, "I'll go and heal him." But the centurion felt unworthy to have Jesus come into his home.

He believed Jesus had authority over sickness just like the authority a centurion has over the men he commands. Jesus was amazed at the faith of the centurion. He said, "Go! It will be done just as you believed it would." And the Bible tells us his servant was healed at that very hour.

"Go! It will be done."

Zacchaeus

On their way to Jerusalem, Jesus and His disciples came to the city of Jericho. It was the home of a very rich man named Zacchaeus. He was the chief tax collector and not liked by the people.

He was the chief tax collector.

Zacchaeus wanted to see Jesus, but he was a very short man and could not see over the crowds. So he climbed up in a sycamore tree. From there he could see Jesus. When Jesus saw Zacchaeus, He said, "Come down, for I am going to stay at your house today." At once, Zacchaeus jumped down from the tree and welcomed Jesus into his home.

When the people saw Jesus being kind to Zacchaeus, they were very upset. They didn't know that Zacchaeus had changed! He said to Jesus, "I'm sorry for the way I have treated the people. I will pay back each one." Jesus was very happy and replied, "Today you are saved, and that is why I have come ... to save the lost!"

"Today you are saved!"

The Triumphal Entry

On Sunday, Jesus came to the Mount of Olives, which is near Jerusalem. He sent two disciples ahead and told them, "As you enter the village, you will find a donkey which no one has ever ridden. Untie it and bring it to Me. If anyone asks what you are doing, say 'The Lord needs it.'"

The disciples obeyed Jesus and brought the donkey to Him.

They spread their coats over the donkey and put Jesus on his back. As Jesus approached Jerusalem, a huge crowd lined the road. Many spread their coats across the road and waved palm branches as if to welcome a hero! Together they shouted, "Hosanna to the King. Blessed is He who comes in the name of the Lord!"

"Hosanna to the King!"

A House of Prayer

On Monday, Jesus entered the temple in Jerusalem. He became very angry at the money changers and those buying and selling doves in God's house. He overturned their tables and drove them all out of the temple . Then He began to teach, "Is it not written, 'My house shall be called a house of prayer?' You have made it a robber's house!" When the priests heard what Jesus had done, they wanted rid of Him.

He overturned the tables.

Worried About Jesus

On Tuesday, Jesus awoke and returned to Jerusalem. Once again, He was greeted by huge crowds who followed Him everywhere. The religious leaders began to worry. "What if Jesus leads the people against us? We could lose our power. We must stop Him!"

They said, "Let's trick Jesus into saying something bad about Rome. Then Rome will arrest Him, and we'll be done with Him!"

"Let's trick Jesus."

Thirty Pieces of Silver

That night Judas Iscariot, one of the twelve disciples, went in to see these church leaders. "I know that you want Jesus removed," he said. "What will you give me if I help you?" They counted out thirty pieces of silver. Judas agreed and started planning to betray Jesus.

Judas betrayed Jesus.

239

The Upper Room

THE UPPER ROOM *Luke 22*

On Thursday evening, Jesus and His twelve disciples met in an upper room to celebrate the Passover. The meal was prepared by Peter and John. He taught them many things that evening. He said that being "the greatest" meant that we must serve others. Then He washed their feet as an example of what a servant does. When it came time to eat, Jesus took some bread, blessed it and gave it to His disciples saying, "Take this bread and eat it; for it is My body." And they all ate.

Then taking the cup, He gave thanks and said, "This is My blood, which is spilled out for many. Do this in remembrance of Me." And they all drank. This was the first communion service.

As the mealtime ended, Jesus spoke once more. "Tonight, I am giving you a new commandment. Love one another. If you do this, everyone will know you are My disciples." They sang a song and together they went back to the Mount of Olives.

PRAYER IN THE GARDEN *Luke 22*

Now there was a beautiful garden near the Mount of Olives called Gethsemane. Jesus and His disciples went there late Thursday night. Jesus said to them, "Sit here while I go and pray." He took Peter, James, and John with Him.

Prayer in the Garden

"My heart is about to break with sorrow," Jesus told them. "Please stay awake and keep watch for Me." Then Jesus walked a little further and fell to the ground praying.

"Father, if it is possible, let these terrible things which are about to happen go away. Yet I am willing to do what You want, not what I want."

"Let these terrible things go away."

Sleepy Disciples

And Jesus prayed so very hard that the sweat on His forehead became drops of blood falling to the ground.

When He returned to His disciples, He found them all asleep. Jesus returned to pray a second and third time. But each time He found his disciples sleeping. Then Jesus knew the worst was about to happen. "Look," He said, "My betrayer is coming!"

"My betrayer is coming."

The Betrayer Comes

Through the darkness and down the narrow pathway came a mob of people carrying torches and clubs. Following was a small group of Roman soldiers. Judas was leading the way. He had told the mob to grab the one he would kiss and to take Him away.

With the mob behind him, Judas stood face to face with Jesus. "Master," said Judas. Then he kissed Jesus. The mob grabbed Him.

The mob grabbed Jesus.

Peter Swings His Sword

Peter pulled out his sword. While trying to protect Jesus, he swung and cut off the ear of one of the chief priest's guards. "Put away the sword!" shouted Jesus. Then Jesus reached out, touched, and healed the servant's ear. There in the darkness the Roman soldiers and the Jewish leaders bound Jesus and took Him away. The disciples were afraid and fled into the night.

Jesus healed the servant's ear.

THE TRIALS OF JESUS
Luke 22-23; Matthew 27

Early Friday morning the many trials of Jesus began.
People lied to judges about things Jesus had said and
done. He was spat upon, beaten, and terribly abused.

When Judas saw what was happening to Jesus, he was
filled with sorrow. He knew he had sinned. He went to
the temple and begged them to release Jesus, but they
would not listen. Judas threw his coins on the temple
floor and ran away. He could no longer live with
himself knowing what he had done to Jesus.

Finally, Jesus was brought before Pontius Pilate, the
Roman governor and judge. The Jewish leaders kept
saying things that were untrue. "He says that He is a
king. And He says we should not pay taxes to Caesar!"
Pilate looked at Jesus, who had been badly beaten, and
asked, "Are You the King of the Jews?" Jesus replied,
"My kingdom is not in this world."

"Then You are a king?" asked Pilate again. "You say
correctly that I am a king," answered Jesus. "But I
come to this world to tell people the truth."

"What is truth?" asked Pilate. Then he said, "I find no
wrong in this man. Let him go."

"My Kingdom is not of this world." 245

Let Them Choose

Each year during the Passover celebration the Roman governor would release one prisoner. The people would decide which one. Pilate knew that the Jewish leaders were accusing Jesus because they were jealous of Him. "The people love Jesus," he thought. "So I'll let them choose between Jesus and that terrible murderer named Barabbas. Surely the people will choose Jesus!"

They would release one prisoner.

So Pilate spoke to the crowd that had gathered. "Should Jesus be set free, or Barabbas?" To Pilate's surprise, he heard them shouting "Barabbas! Free Barabbas!"

"What shall I do with Jesus?" Pilate asked the crowd. "Kill Him! Crucify Him!" they shouted. Louder and louder their cries rang out until Pilate, fearing a riot, decided to please them.

Affirmation: I will choose Jesus to be my savior!

"Crucify him!", they shouted.

The Crucifixion

Jesus was then turned over to the Roman soldiers. They stripped off His clothes and beat Him with a whip. They made fun of Him by putting a purple robe on His back and placing a crown of thorns on His head.

Jesus was silent. Then they put His own clothes back on Him and led Him away to a place called Golgotha to be crucified.

They made fun of Jesus.

On Friday morning they crucified Jesus and two lawbreakers, one on the right and the other on the left. As Jesus hung on the cross He was heard to say, "Father forgive them, for they do not know what they are doing."

Then one of the lawbreakers hanging with Jesus said, "If you really are the King of the Jews, save Yourself!" But the other lawbreaker said, "Be quiet! We deserve to die because we have done many bad things. This man has done nothing wrong. Jesus, remember me."

"Father, forgive them."

A Borrowed Tomb

Jesus looked at this man and said, "Today you will be with Me in heaven." A great darkness fell over the land for three hours. Jesus cried out from the cross with a loud voice, "It is finished! Father, I give to You My Spirit." And having said this, He died.

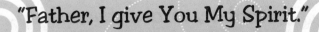
"Father, I give You My Spirit."

Jesus' body was placed in the borrowed tomb of a secret disciple named Joseph. They rolled a large stone in front of the opening and went away.

On Sunday morning, a woman named Mary Magdalene and the other Mary came to the tomb. They found the giant stone had been rolled away. Upon the stone sat an angel who said, "Jesus is not here. He is alive! Quickly now, go tell His disciples."

The stone has been rolled away.

Jesus Has Risen

They ran like the wind to tell the disciples. "Jesus has risen! He's alive!" They were so happy!

Jesus appeared to many people. He walked with two followers on the Emmaus Road. Then Jesus visited the disciples in Jerusalem as they gathered to eat supper. "Peace be with you," Jesus said. He ate with them and showed them His nail-scarred hands and feet.

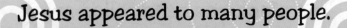

Jesus appeared to many people.

Jesus was truly alive ... He had risen from the grave!
"Remember what I said on the way to Jerusalem several days ago? 'I will be handed over to the Roman leaders. I will be unkindly treated and, just like the prophets said, I will die and on the third day I will come back to life again.' All these things you have now seen."

Jesus was truly alive.

The Great Commission

"Now you must go into every nation and tell them the good news of God's coming kingdom. Tell them that if they believe in Me and My words, they will live forever, just like Me!"

Jesus stayed with the disciples a while longer. Then after He had blessed each of them, He said, "I am going now to live with My Father and your Father. Be sure that I am always going to be with you."

Jesus is always with us.

Up, Up and Away

Then Jesus rose up into the air until He disappeared in the clouds.

As they were gazing into the sky, two men in white clothing stood beside them and said, "One day Jesus will come again in this very same way." Then the disciples returned to Jerusalem to start their ministries.

One day Jesus will come again.

Stephen Forgave

Stephen was a leader in the early church. He was full of God's power. Everywhere he went, he did great miracles and told everyone that Jesus is God's son. The people began to follow Jesus, which made the religious leaders angry. Even though Stephen did nothing wrong, the religious leaders decided to kill him!

Stephen told everyone about God's love and how He had forgiven the sins of Adam and Eve, Moses and David. He forgives everyone who believes in Him! Even as the people were throwing stones to kill him, Stephen asked God to forgive them.

He was full of God's power.

Blinded by the Light

Many of the Jewish religious leaders continued to treat the Christian believers in a very unkind way. Saul of Tarsus was probably the most unkind. He did not believe in the Lord Jesus. He had men and women who loved the Lord put in chains and taken away to terrible prisons.

Christians were put into chains.

One day as Saul and his friends were traveling to a city called Damascus, a very bright light suddenly shone around him. Then Saul heard a voice from heaven saying, "Saul, why are you so unkind to Me?" When Saul asked, "Who are You, Lord?" He heard the voice reply, "I am Jesus." Then Saul knew that Jesus really was alive!

The light was so brilliant that it blinded Saul. Trembling with fear Saul asked, "Lord, what do you want me to do?"

The Lord commanded him to go to Damascus, and Saul obeyed.

"Lord, what do you want me to do?"

Three dark days later, God sent a good man named Ananias to visit Saul. Suddenly, he could see again! Saul praised God as Ananias told him about God's special plan for his life. Later, Saul even changed his name from Saul to Paul, for now he would live for Jesus.

Saul changed his name to Paul.

The Romans Road

Paul was a letter writer. He wrote very special letters to the Christian churches of his time. Some of Paul's letters are in our Holy Bible ... like his letter to the Romans. In this letter, he tells us we can be saved by following these steps:

Romans 3:23 -For everyone has sinned and fallen short of the glory of God.

Romans 6:23 -For the wages of sin is death, but the gift of God is eternal life through Jesus Christ our Lord.

Romans 5:8 -But God showed His love for us in this way: while we were still sinners, Christ died for us.

Romans 10:10 -For it is with your heart that you believe and with your mouth that you confess and are saved.

Romans 10:13 -For everyone who calls on the name of the Lord will be saved.

Paul's wonderful letter to the Romans shows us how to lead a friend to Jesus.

Affirmation: I will lead a friend to Jesus!

Christ died for you and me.

Dorcas Gave to Those in Need

Dorcas was a follower of Jesus. She was known throughout Joppa for her kindness and generosity. One day, Dorcas became ill and died. Her friends sent for Peter to comfort her family and friends. When Peter arrived, the widows stood around him, crying and showing him the clothes Dorcas had made for them.

Peter knelt before Dorcas and prayed. Then he said to her, "Dorcas, get up!" And she sat up! She was alive! Dorcas had given her life to serving others. Now God had given life to her.

God had given life to her!

God's Kind of Love

There was a brand new group of Christians who started a church in the great city of Corinth, Greece. Corinth was full of idol worshipers and Paul had journeyed there many times to preach the good news of Jesus Christ. In one of his letters written to this growing church, he explained the meaning of "God's kind of Love." He wrote: "If I could speak with the words of an angel, but had no love inside my heart, I would only be making noise like a clanging cymbal.

Paul preached the Good News!

If I knew all there was to know and could move mountains with my faith, I would still have an empty heart without love. If I gave everything I own to the poor, I would gain nothing if it wasn't given in love. When we have God's kind of love in our hearts, we are willing to be patient with others. When we have God's kind of love in our hearts, we don't become jealous of others, wanting what they may have.

God's love makes us patient and kind.

When we have God's kind of love in our hearts, we never hurt anyone's feelings by being rude, and we always forgive others. When we have God's love in our hearts, we think of others first, not ourselves. We stay away from bad things and seek to do good things. When we have God's kind of love inside, we protect the helpless, and hope for the good. God's kind of love keeps on loving no matter what happens. That's why God's love is the greatest gift we can give to others."

God's love is the greatest of all gifts.

Yoked Together

Several years after Paul had written his first letter to the Corinthians, the church began to have many problems. A missionary named Titus was sent by Paul to help the church grow. Titus was a great teacher and soon the people returned to God's way of doing things. When Titus returned with his good report, Paul was so excited!

Titus helped the church grow.

Guided by the Holy Spirit, Paul wrote a second letter. His words tell us how to keep from falling into sin.

"Do not join a group of people who do not share your belief in Jesus. For what do good deeds and bad deeds have in common? What kind of friendship can light have with darkness? What do the teachings of Jesus and Satan have in common? What does a believer and an unbeliever have in common? Because you are a Christian, separate yourself from those who do bad things and God will be a Father to you and you will be His sons and daughters."

Affirmation: I want to have Christian friends!

God will be a Father to you.

The Fruit of the Spirit

The missionary Paul wrote many letters to the early churches. He wrote this one to the church at Galatia. Like the Corinthians, they too were following false teachers who thought that good works alone made you a Christian. But we know that only faith in Jesus Christ makes us a Christian.

Paul's letter of love to the Galatians read as follows: People of Galatia, God does not measure us by the works of our hands. The only thing that matters is faith, and the love we give to others by faith.

Faith in Jesus makes us a Christian.

So I say, let the Holy Spirit guide you and when He does, your life will bring forth fruit just like a fruit tree. But the fruit of the Spirit will be

LOVE
JOY
PEACE
PATIENCE
KINDNESS
GOODNESS
FAITHFULNESS
GENTLENESS
SELF-CONTROL

Let the Holy Spirit help you to be a fruitful person!

Affirmation: I will let the Holy Spirit guide me!

Rhoda Served with Joy

She worked long hours for John Mark's mother, Mary. Mary was a wealthy widow who opened her home to believers. One night, believers had gathered there to pray. Suddenly there was a knock at the door.

When Rhoda heard Peter's voice, her joy overflowed. She ran to tell the others. She was so excited, she forgot to open the door and let Peter in! When they opened the door, there stood Peter. Rhoda's joy was contagious. Everyone was full of joy.

She forgot to open the door.

Children Obey

Paul's letter to the church at Ephesus included some words just for children. Children, obey your parents in the Lord for this is right. Honor your father and mother which is the first commandment with a promise. God promises that things will be well with you and you will enjoy a long life on the earth.

Paul went on to explain that as followers of Jesus we are soldiers in the Lord's army. Satan is the enemy we fight.

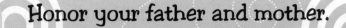

Honor your father and mother.

So put on the whole armor of God. He gave these examples. Put on a *BELT OF TRUTH* and a *BREASTPLATE OF RIGHTEOUSNESS*. Cover your feet with the *GOSPEL OF PEACE*. Take up a *SHIELD OF FAITH* to protect you from Satan's fiery arrows. Put on the *HELMET OF SALVATION* and the *SWORD OF THE SPIRIT* which is the Bible. And pray about each decision and pray for your friends. Being a soldier isn't always fun, but God's army needs you every day to fight the good fight!

Put on the belt of Truth.

Think About These Things

Once again Paul dips his pen into the ink and writes another letter. This time he addresses it to the believers in Philippi. "Thank you," he writes, "for all the many ways you have helped the cause of Christ. And be sure of this, that He who began a good work in you will help you to complete it. Our God is faithful. So continue to work without complaining or arguing and live together in peace. That way you will shine like stars in the universe."

"Our God is Faithful."

"And finally brothers and sisters, whatever is true, whatever is noble, whatever is right, whatever is pure, whatever is lovely, whatever is admirable, think about these things. Practice what you preach and the God of peace will be with you. For this, friends, is the secret to being happy: we can do all things through Christ who strengthens us!"

Affirmation: I can do all things through Christ who strengthens me!

"We can do all things through Christ!"

Heart-Working People

Paul taught the believers in the Colossian church that they had been rescued, much like a drowning man. Except we were rescued from the evil one and brought into God's kingdom. It's like being born again, for had we not been rescued and saved we would have died. Now we rejoice and we live for Jesus.

We live for Jesus!

So whatever you do, work at it with all your heart as working for the Lord and not for men. For it is the Lord you are serving. Make the most of every opportunity God gives you. Do your very best!

Affirmation: I will do my very best at all times!

Make the most of every opportunity.

Every Day is Pray Day!

Paul had a great love and pleasant memories of the church in Thessalonica. Their faith and love of God had grown even while they were being treated very harshly. They shared the Word of God with others and they lived it every day. They believed, as we do, that Jesus is alive and someday He is coming back to this earth to claim us as His people. Because of this wonderful news, Paul writes, "Rejoice always, pray without ceasing, and in everything give thanks!"

In everything give thanks!

The Day of the Lord

In Paul's second letter to the Thessalonians he warns the believer that false teachers would come into the church. He writes, "Beware! These teachers will be able to work certain kinds of miracles. But Satan is the source of their power. So pray for us that we may escape their evil traps. For we know the Lord is faithful, and He will strengthen and protect us from the evil one."

Affirmation: The Lord will strengthen and protect me!

We know the Lord is faithful!

The Example

In a letter to his dear friend Timothy, Paul tells him to be about God's work, which is saving lost sinners. We are also to pray for the leaders of our country.

Then Paul writes some very important words, "For there is one God, and one peacemaker who stands between God and men; that man is Jesus Christ who gave Himself as a payment for our sin. This is the gospel message to young and old. Therefore, let no one look down on you because you are young; but rather set an example for those who believe."

"For there is only one God."

A Special Letter

Paul wrote a second letter to his missionary friend Timothy. In it, God tells us that all scripture in our Holy Bible is given by inspiration of the Holy Spirit. It is profitable for teaching and for training people to live holy lives. These precious Bible verses make us spiritually ready to do the work of God. Some may preach the Word. Some may teach, but all must serve. The Bible says that a day is soon coming when many people will no longer believe in God. Let us therefore, work today, for the hour is late.

Affirmation: I will serve the Lord!

Some may preach, but all must serve!

Mercy, Mercy Me

Once a young pastor in the ancient city of Crete opened a letter sent to him by Paul. It was a very short, but powerful letter. It read, "Teach the people of Crete the truth of God's word. Teach the older men to be self-controlled and to love one another. Teach the older women to live in a loving and kind way, never harming others with unkind or untrue words." Jesus wanted them to set an example for younger Christians.

And always remember, God saved us not because of righteous things we had done, but because of His mercy. So please learn to do what is good in His sight.

Grace be with you!

Do what is good in His sight.

Onesimus

Paul was arrested for preaching the gospel while in the city of Rome. This letter was written from his prison cell to a wealthy friend named Philemon. Philemon had a slave named Onesimus who had stolen from him and run away to Rome to hide. But while there, Onesimus met Paul and gave his heart to Jesus. He then decided to return to his master to make things right again.

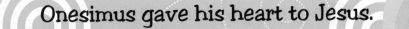

Onesimus gave his heart to Jesus.

So Paul writes, "I thank God always, making mention of you in my prayers." Then he explained that Onesimus was no longer a slave, but a brother in Christ. He asked Philemon to welcome Onesimus home as he would welcome Paul himself. "If he has done you any wrong," Paul writes, "or if he owes you any money, charge it to me and I will pay it back." Paul loved Onesimus and prayed for his safe return.

Paul prayed for Onesimus.

The Hall of Faith

What does faith mean? It is believing what God says in his Word and acting on it. "For without faith, it is impossible to please God."

The book of Hebrews presents a list of ordinary men and women who became heroes of faith.

Let's take a tour of God's Hall of Faith found in the book of Hebrews.

JOSEPH

MOSES SARAH

JACOB

ISAAC ENOCH

NOAH

RAHAB

ABEL

ABRAHAM

ABEL: By faith Abel offered God a blood sacrifice which pleased Him.

NOAH: By faith Noah obeyed God, building an ark miles from any sea.

ABRAHAM: By faith Abraham left his home for a place God would show him.

SARAH: By faith Sarah believed God's promise and had a baby at age 90.

ISAAC: By faith Isaac passed the promises of God on to his sons.

ABRAHAM

JOSEPH

SARAH

NOAH

JACOB: By faith Jacob, as he was dying, blessed the sons of Joseph.

JOSEPH: By faith Joseph commanded his bones be taken to Canaan where God would fulfill His promise.

MOSES: By faith Moses believed God, choosing to suffer with the people of God.

RAHAB: By faith Rahab believed that Israel's God was true and hid the spies.

JACOB

ISAAC

My picture here

_____
My name

RAHAB

MOSES

Affirmation: My faith is going to grow!

The Lord's Brother

The book of James was written by Jesus' brother, James. At first, James did not believe in Jesus. But after Jesus rose from the dead, he believed and wrote this wonderful book on faith. "Take note," he writes, "everyone should be quick to listen, slow to speak, and slow to become angry. But do not listen only; do what God's Word says!

Do what God's Word says.

And remember, your tongue is like the rudder on a large sailing ship. Even though a ship is large and driven by strong winds, it is steered by a very small rudder. In the very same way, our tongues are small, but they can make big boasts.

Out of the same mouth we can praise God and say bad things. This should not be. Can fresh water and salt water flow from the same spring? Neither should our tongues praise and say bad things."

The Humble Never Crumble

Peter addressed his wonderful letter to God's chosen people. He calls us "strangers in this world." Now strangers are people who have a home somewhere else. They're just visiting for a while. Peter knew that a Christian's true home is in heaven. We live here as "strangers," seeking first the things of God, not the things of gold and glory. This is very strange indeed to worldly people.

Our home is in Heaven.

But Peter says, "Humble yourselves under God's mighty hand. This means we should set aside our own wants and wishes and do the things that please God. Be self-controlled; for our enemy, Satan, prowls around as a roaring lion, just looking for someone to hurt. Resist him, stand firm in the faith, and he will flee from you. We are truly strangers here, but someday soon we'll be going home to heaven."

Be self-controlled; obey God!

A Simple Reminder

Has anyone ever written you a reminder note? Peter writes his second letter as a friendly reminder note to all believers.

"If we follow Jesus, we will never fail." This is a promise of God!

"So be good Christians having self-control, kindness, and brotherly love. And be faithful to memorize the words spoken by the prophets. Each day, think about the commands of Jesus Christ. If we do these things, we will grow. We will grow in grace and in the knowledge of our Lord and Savior Jesus Christ."

Walking with God

John tells us that if we are to walk with God, we must walk in the light. For God is light. We are to be honest when we speak and loving to those in need. If we walk in the light, Satan, that prince of darkness, can never harm us. John also reminds us that God is love. "Dear children, let us not love with words, but with actions and truth." If we walk in the light and in His love, surely we will walk with Jesus forever in heaven.

That's a mighty promise!

Affirmation:
I will walk
with Jesus!

Walk in the Light!

Never Too Young!

In John's second letter, he writes to an unnamed woman and her children. John loved children very much ... just like Jesus. John was so happy to learn these children were walking with Jesus. "Love one another," he writes, "and this is love: that we walk according to Jesus' commandments."

Each child is very special. Each of you have a very important work to do in God's kingdom. Remember, you're never too young to love one another.

Love one another!

I've Got Hospitality

In John's third letter he writes to his dear Christian friend named Gaius. He says many kind things to Gaius to encourage him. Gaius was living his life in a way that pleased Jesus. Perhaps his greatest gift was that of hospitality. He would always take care of the missionaries who came to visit his church. He made sure they had a warm meal and a place to sleep. We, too, ought to show hospitality to our Christian friends and workers.

Show hospitality to our Christian friends!

Beware!

Sometimes we must fight for what we believe in. Jude, the other brother of Jesus, warns us in this short letter to beware of godless men and women who secretly slip into our churches. Remember, if anyone denies that Jesus is the Son of God, that person is not teaching the truth.

We stand up for Jesus. We put on the armor of faith and march into battle. Using the sword of the Spirit, we fight the good fight!

For the victory has already been won at Calvary. Therefore keep yourselves in the love of God.

Stand up, stand up for Jesus.

The Book of Life

It's wonderful to know that we serve a living Savior. He is at this very moment preparing our homes in heaven. And one day soon, Jesus will break through the clouds and come back to this earth to claim His children. Satan, that old serpent, will be defeated. Then comes the greatest moment in history when Jesus opens the "Lamb's Book of Life."

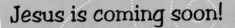

Jesus is coming soon!

If you have asked Jesus to come into
your heart, your name
will be written in the
Lamb's Book of Life.

Just think ... God knows your
name, and has heard your
prayers. If you've never
asked Jesus into your
heart, but you
want to,
just pray this little prayer:

*Dear Heavenly Father, I believe that Jesus died on
a cross for me, and I believe He rose again and lives
today. Please forgive me of all my sins and let
Jesus come into my heart. Amen.*

GLOSSARY

Altar – a place where gifts are brought to God

Angel – a messenger sent from heaven

Ark – a place of protection, like the big boat Noah built

Ark of the Covenant – the box used to carry the original copy of the Ten Commandments

Armor – a covering that protects you

Banquet – a special dinner to honor a person or event

Baptize – act of dunking under water as an outward sign of faith in Jesus

Begotten – born into a family

Birthright – the honor or blessing given to a first born son

Blessing – a prayer or wish for happiness, health, and good fortune

Breastplate – a covering worn to protect the chest

Caravan – a group of people following each other on a trip

Comfort – to help another person when they are sad or sick

Covet – to want something that is not yours

Crucify – to hang someone on a "T" shaped post until they die

Descendant – what you are to your parents and what your parents are to your grandparents

Deliverance – to be made safe from danger or harm

Disciple – a follower who learns from the person they follow

Faith – to believe or trust something even though you cannot see it

Famine – a time when there is little or no food

Forgive – excusing someone who has done something you don't like

Gallows – the name of the place where people are hanged

Gentleness – to be very kind a polite to others

Glean – to gather grain, like wheat, that has been left in a field

Goodness – being very kind

Gospel – good news

Grace – something good that you didn't work for or deserve

Guidance – showing someone how to do something

Helmet – a covering to protect the head

Holy – something or someone set apart for God

Hospitality – to welcome visitors and treat them very nice

Humble – not thinking you are better than anyone else

Idol – anything you make more important than God

Invisible – something that cannot be seen with your eyes

Joy – a feeling of happiness

Judge – to decide what happens to someone based on the law

Kindness – when you are fair and nice

Locust – an insect that looks like a grasshopper

Manger – an open box used to feed animals like horses and cows

Manna – a kind of bread God sent from heaven

Mercy – to show someone forgiveness

Miracle – something that cannot be explained

Missionary – a person who tells others about Jesus

Mock – to make fun of someone in a mean way

Mourn – to be very sad, especially when someone dies

Noble – when you are very important or have great courage

Offering – a gift gladly given

Parable – a story that teaches a lesson

Patience – being able to wait without being in a hurry

Peace – feeling good inside or a time of quiet

Perish – to die

Pillar – a tall post or column

Plague – when a lot of people have the same bad trouble or illness

Praise – telling how much you like someone or something

Pray – to speak to God

Preach – telling a message or news to other people

Priest – a person who has a special relationship with God

Prison – a place to lock someone inside, especially when they have broken the law

Proclaim – to make an announcement

Prophet – someone God asks to tell others about him or to deliver a special message

Protect – to keep safe or keep from getting hurt

Pure – something that is perfect with no mistakes

Remnant – the part or piece that is left

Repent – to say you're sorry and ask forgiveness

Rescue – to set free or keep from being hurt

Revelation – to make something known that has been hidden

Righteous – to do what is right

Sacrifice – to give away something as a gift

Salvation – what God gives to anyone to wants to be a part of his family

Savior – someone who saves us from something bad; in the Bible, Jesus is called Savior because he saves us from our sins

Scripture – sentences and verses from the Bible

Seek – to look for something

Self-control – to be able to keep yourself from doing wrong

Serpent – a reptile, usually a snake

Servant – a person who works for someone else

Shield – a piece of armor used to protect and keep you safe

Slavery – when one person is owned by another person

Slingshot – a stick with a leather strap used to throw rocks or stones

Staff – a tall cane or stick someone carries to help them walk

Swaddling – strips of cloth wrapped around a newborn baby

Sword – a weapon with a sharp blade and a handle

Taxes – extra fees or money people have to pay to their government

Temple – the special building where people go to worship God

Tomb – a grave, or a place where the dead are buried

Victory – when you win

Wicked – very bad

Wise – to be very smart, and use knowledge to make good decisions

Worship – to love and honor